PRIMARY GAMES

STEVE **SUGAR**

KIM KOSTOROSKI **SUGAR**

PRIMARY GAMES

Experiential **Learning**
Activities for **Teaching**
Children **K-8**

JOSSEY-BASS
A Wiley Company
www.josseybass.com

Published by

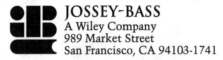

JOSSEY-BASS
A Wiley Company
989 Market Street
San Francisco, CA 94103-1741

www.josseybass.com

Jossey-Bass books and products are available through most bookstores. To contact Jossey-Bass directly, call (888) 378-2537, fax to (800) 605-2665, or visit our website at www.josseybass.com.

Substantial discounts on bulk quantities of Jossey-Bass books are available to corporations, professional associations, and other organizations. For details and discount information, contact the special sales department at Jossey-Bass.

We at Jossey-Bass strive to use the most environmentally sensitive paper stocks available to us. Our publications are printed on acid-free recycled stock whenever possible, and our paper always meets or exceeds minimum GPO and EPA requirements.

Library of Congress Cataloging-in-Publication Data
Sugar, Steve.
Primary games: experiential learning activities for teaching
children K-8 / Steve Sugar, Kim Kostoroski Sugar.—1st ed.
p. cm.—(The Jossey-Bass education series)
ISBN 0–7879–6081–0 (alk. paper)
1. Educational games. 2. Activity programs in education. 3.
Experiential learning. I. Sugar, Kim Kostoroski, 1975- II.
Title. III. Series.
LB1029.G3 S92 2002
371.33'7—dc21   2002003254

FIRST EDITION

PB Printing   10 9 8 7 6 5 4 3 2 1

The Jossey-Bass Education Series

CONTENTS

PART TWO # Twenty-Five Games

PART **THREE** # FINDING THE RIGHT GAME

This book is dedicated to

all educators who create the future every day in their classrooms.

PREFACE

The Sesame Street experience has taught us this—
if you can hold the attention of children,
you can educate them.

—Malcolm Gladwell, *The Tipping Point*

The games in this book bring the joy of learning back into the classroom. These games create a cognitive engagement between the student and the topic in a flowing, smiling environment—where successes are memorable moments of shared triumph and celebration and where mistakes mean only that the student is being stretched to her or his own limits. These games and activities help you—the classroom or at-home educator—celebrate the topic and reward individual achievement. These games are meant to bring fun into the classroom, but with the focus on learning. . . "fun with a purpose."

THE BENEFITS OF GAMES

Learning games engage students and then motivate them to interact with the topic. This interaction drives players to demonstrate their understanding of the topic in a friendly competition against themselves, other players, and the time and scoring standards. Moreover, during this play, players practice the social skills of communication, collaboration, and following instructions, as well as cognitive skills such as problem solving and critical thinking. One particularly exciting thing about the games in this book is that they can be used in the classroom or one-on-one. The classroom teacher, the parent who home schools, and the caregiver who wants to give her child extra help at home will find these games very helpful.

The Benefits of Games: A Personal Success Story

The fourth-grader quietly entered the apartment and put away his books. Without a word he went to his room. Because he was usually cheerful and energetic after school, his mother was troubled.

When asked, the boy said that the teacher was "out to get him." After a few gentle questions the real culprit was revealed—fractions. The boy had to solve several homework problems for the next class. When the mother tried to explain fractions, the boy became upset. Even a demonstration with cut-up circles and squares did not help to introduce the new topic.

Nothing was mentioned during dinner. After dinner the mother drew a game sheet for the boy's favorite game, Tic-Tac-Toe, on a sheet of paper. They quickly became involved in play. After a couple of rounds the mother introduced a change in the rules—to cover a space on the game sheet the boy would have to answer a question. Eager to continue, he stayed and played. Starting with easy questions, the mother reviewed some math he already knew. Then she introduced fractions into the question mix. As play continued the boy began to understand fractions. He also realized that fractions were not as difficult as he had thought. When play was over, the boy quickly completed his homework assignment.

The next day he returned to the classroom confident and ready to build on what he had learned about the material through play. And so began a lifelong relationship between one of the authors and learning games.

WHAT'S IN IT FOR YOU?

This book presents a wonderful collection of games that will engage your student through a variety of formats. Here is a sample of what this book brings to your curriculum and audience:

Celebrate the Topic

These games celebrate any curriculum topic by positioning the topic information in a zone where children experience playful learning. These games bring fun to a topic, and when it's fun to learn, children love learning.

Play Great Games

This book contains a collection of twenty-five of the most distinctive and playful content-reinforcing designs available anywhere. These games will increase the *smile quotient* of any audience. Many of these game formats are already well known and loved by your students, including

- Classic favorites: crossword, bingo, and tic-tac-toe
- Sports favorites: baseball, basketball, golf, and Olympic races
- Prop favorites: bubble makers, balloons, and cut-up shapes
- TV game shows
- Classic children's games

Customize Games Easily

These game formats are open to any topic material and can be adapted to any level of use. Each game allows you to place your material into the game format, like placing a picture into an open picture frame, and then you can immediately play it with your audience. Each game includes complete instructions, scoring examples, and tips on how you can customize it with your material and to your audience.

Offer One-on-One Tutoring

Each of these games can be easily adapted to special tutoring situations in class or at home. These games will bring the learning home to the most hard-to-please student.

Keep Students Active as They Learn

Games are an active way to keep your students involved in the curriculum; they keep your students on their toes. Imagine juggling a balloon while learning, or blowing bubbles while learning, or tossing paper trash balls while learning. These games keep children energized while learning.

Encourage Social Bonding

Playing in teams gives children a chance to know their peers. Game playing allows for strong social bonding, an important part of the school experience.

Develop Tools That Travel Well

Most teachers do not stay in the same grade and teach the same curriculum for their entire career. These games accompany you to whatever grade or curriculum awaits. Just wrap the game around your new curriculum, and you instantly have a fun activity for your students.

Complement Your Teaching Plan

These games can be used with your current teaching plan. The time required ranges from ten to fifty minutes, and many games require minimum setup and breakdown. In addition these games are flexible enough to be used in almost any time slot. They can introduce a topic or class day, refocus students returning from an active recess, review information presented earlier, or bring closure to the class day.

Let Students Play and Learn

Play is a crucial element in developing the whole child, especially in the early elementary years when play can be a child's most important work. Games are the perfect vehicle to bring the fun and energy of play into a learning zone.

THE BOOK AT A GLANCE

This book is intended for immediate use. The layout encourages you to search out one or more games that meet your needs and then adapt them to your curriculum. Moreover, we have included many features designed to help you find the right game and adapt it to your needs.

Part One: Connecting Games to Learning

Chapter One: How Games Can Promote Learning

This chapter discusses how games can be used to satisfy the learning styles of your students and then looks at fourteen ways games bring learning to your classroom.

Chapter Two: Selecting an Appropriate Game

This chapter offers tips on selecting your game in terms of target audience, learning outcomes, and playing time. The chapter closes with an overview of modifying your game in terms of class size, time of play, focus of the task, and scoring.

Chapter Three: Developing Game Content

This chapter focuses on the development of your learning game. Topics include the process of "loading," or placing, your content into your game, three loading techniques, eight question writing tips, six sample question formats, and ways to immediately involve your game with existing lesson material.

Chapter Four: Setting Up and Running a Game

This chapter covers the physical and mental preparation needed to set up and play a classroom game. Topics include selection and use of game accessories, game setup, game preliminaries, game play, and closing.

Part Two: Twenty-Five Games

- Activity Cards: card question-and-answer game

- Alphabet Soup: team word-forming game

- At Risk: small-group question-and-response game

- Balloon Juggle: multitask game

- Batter Up!: baseball question-and-answer game

- Bingo 1: Letter Bingo: letter identification game

- Bingo 2: Math Bingo: number identification game

- Bingo 3: Wall Bingo: TV-format wall game

- Bits and Pieces: team task game

- Bubbles: bubble-making game

- Crosswords: word-solving game

- Dilemma: team sorting game

- Fast Track: team wall chart game

- Grab Bag: team question-and-reward game

- Granny Squares: question-and-cover game

- Guesstimate: team test challenge game

- Guggenheim: team creativity game

- Knowledge Golf: team problem-solving game

- Lightning Round: team rapid-fire question-and-answer game

- Medley Relay: team task relay game

- Music Time: team question-and-answer game

- Scavenger Hunt: individual or team clue-solving game

- Spin Off: individual or team question-and-answer game

- Three-in-a-Row: Tic-Tac-Toe question-and-answer game

- Trash Ball: basketball toss-and-answer game

For each game we present an introductory overview and then describe the game's purpose and objective and its logistics: the number of players and their grade level, the approximate time of play, and the supplies required. Then we lay out, step by step, how to play and score the game. Finally, we supply detailed teacher notes, tips on customizing the game, and a page of player instructions that can be made into an overhead transparency.

Part Three: Finding the Right Game

Appendix One: Game Summaries

This appendix presents an abstract of each game to give you a feel for the game's features and "personality." A quick review of these abstracts should give you many ideas for using these games for your audience and topic.

Appendix Two: Sample Game Lessons

This appendix describes two topic- and grade-related challenges and then presents a six-step game plan that walks you through the preparation of a game specifically tailored to meet each challenge.

Appendix Three: Games for Special Situations

This appendix takes five special situations that challenge most educators, new and experienced alike—the first week of school, test preparation, material review, active days, and learning centers—and lists games that can be used to deal successfully with each challenge at different grade levels.

Appendix Four: Game Match Matrix

This appendix presents a matrix matching each game against the criteria of grade level, curriculum, group size, location in or out of chair, special day activity, learning center activity, and time of play. This matrix can help you find the games you need for your students, plan your next lesson, or adapt to circumstances when you need an instant activity thanks to sudden changes in curriculum, audience, or weather.

Acknowledgments

To Jason, my husband, for the support you always have given me as a mother and a teacher.

To Clarisse and Luke, for showing me that an adult's best teacher is often a child.

To my first teachers—Mom, Dad, and Tim—for showing me that learning can and should be a joyful experience.

To my University of North Carolina friends, Dr. Richard Brice, Dr. Barbara Day, and Beth Althiser, for reinspiring my love for teaching and showing me that educating young people is a true blessing.

K.K.S.

To Marie, my wife and sounding board, for her endless patience during this project. Unpack your suitcase, dear, the book is finally written.

To my mother, Anne, for teaching me how to learn through play (and who predicted that I was destined to grow old before I would grow up)—thanks, from your rapidly aging Peter Pan.

To Sivasailam Thiagarajan, the creative and prolific writer, for encouraging and guiding me through my evolution as a games writer. He was even kind enough to laugh at my jokes. Thanks, Thiagi.

To the many English professors who endured my writings, for introducing me to writing as a form of self-expression—with special thanks to John Wheatcroft of Bucknell University.

To Lesley Iura and Christie Hakim, for making this project a reality.

S. S.

THE AUTHORS

STEVE SUGAR graduated from Bucknell University with a B.S. degree in economics and English. He received his M.B.A. degree from the George Washington University. He teaches management courses for the Economics and Administrative Services program at the University of Maryland Baltimore County (UMBC), an honors university in Maryland. Steve is the author of *Games That Teach* (Jossey-Bass/Pfeiffer, 1998), coauthor of *Games That Teach Teams* (Jossey-Bass/Pfeiffer, 2000), and the developer of five instructional game systems used worldwide. He is also the author of *More Great Games* (ASTD INFO-LINE, 2000) and a frequent contributor to educational and professional journals. Steve has taught courses in instructional game design for the graduate curriculums at Johns Hopkins University and the New York Institute of Technology. He also teaches workshops on the topic of developing and using classroom games at teacher's conferences, colleges, and national organizations.

KIM KOSTOROSKI SUGAR is certified as an elementary teacher in the state of Massachusetts and has served as a technology teacher. She earned her B.A.

degree cum laude in sociology and elementary education from the University of Massachusetts and her M.Ed. degree from the University of North Carolina at Chapel Hill. While at Chapel Hill, she participated in a study of developmentally appropriate practices in the classroom, research on phonics versus whole language as a teaching approach, and an in-depth look at literacy in young children. More generally, her interests established at this time were in infants and their development and parent education and involvement in the classroom. Her work in developing resource files and designing concrete ways to encourage parent involvement in the classroom grew into a workshop given at the Grady Brown Elementary School in Hillsborough, N.C.

Kim is now devoting her time to being a stay-at-home mom, monitoring the literacy Web site she has created, and doing research on home schooling her own children.

PRIMARY GAMES

PART ONE

TEACHING WITH GAMES

CHAPTER ONE

How Games Can Promote Learning

Many people think of learning as "hard work."
Learning, as great teachers have known throughout the ages,
does not *feel* like work when you're having fun.
—Marc Prensky, *Digital Game-Based Learning*

Teachers compete against a world of entertaining distractions in which the best instructional programming seems to incorporate a prescribed mix of eye candy, puppets, storytelling, cartoons, and music. This is a tough act to follow! But mass media cannot deal with our students' needs on a daily and continuing basis. We all know what our students need in terms of curriculum and application, but sometimes we need help in creating the appropriate education-to-entertainment mix that meets their needs on a day-to-day basis.

As educators and parents, we are always looking for ways to engage our students and our children with the classroom topic. Our lessons are not "work" to us, and we certainly don't want them to be "work" to our students. We want our students to *want* to know more about the topic, to become vested in their own learning experience—connecting their own dots and experiencing their own ideas.

The twenty-five games in this book bring students into the learning arena. Each game has a playful feature that intrigues students and transforms them into players who interact with the game format. Once involved in the play of the game, each player actively interacts with the topic and also demonstrates skills in problem solving, creativity, and group dynamics. These games are powerful tools that extend the invitation to all players to "come on in, the learning's fine."

GAMES AND INDIVIDUAL LEARNING STYLES

Each student has a personal preference for how she receives, interprets, and understands information. Michael Grinder, in his book *Righting the Education Conveyor Belt,* divides learners into three main types—visual, auditory, and kinesthetic. As educators we hope to successfully address all three types of learners each day and with each lesson. Games are an amicable way for an educator to present material and assess material learned, in a way that appeals to all her students. Games also help you maximize each student's learning potential. Games help everyone win.

Here are the learning types and the ways games satisfy each type:

- *Visual learners.* Reflective of our visual age, many of our students are visual learners, reacting favorably to reading assignments, pictures, wall charts, overheads, videos, worksheets, game sheets, and other visual media. To these students the props, game sheets, and visual sequences enacted during a game create a visual experience that can be recalled to reinforce the items or concepts covered in the activity.

- *Auditory learners.* Many students react favorably to music, oral stories, reading aloud, class sing-alongs, sounds, class discussions, and ongoing dialogue. For these students the oral directions in games, repeated episodes of question-and-response, and ongoing discussions create a memorable experience.

- *Kinesthetic learners.* Many students prefer to be involved in the learning experience through touch and interaction, as occurs during game play. They like tactile experiences, such as touching ordinary game items like game sheets, pencils, and markers, and may especially enjoy touching special game props, such as balloons, trash balls, chips, letter cards, question cards, and so forth. The actual physical movement involved in certain games is also important for these learners. They will enjoy the out-of-the-chair games. These students especially enjoy interacting with the other students during the socialization required in a competitive game environment. Students become players, and players become teams during the surge of energy and adrenaline that occurs during game play.

Learning types can also be expressed as internal and external styles.

- *Internal learners.* These learners prefer working alone to create a product or solution—they enjoy reflecting and then working out the solutions in their heads before presenting an answer. Games encourage and reward the type of reflection and thought that is needed to provide the best answers.

- *External learners.* These learners are very social and thrive on group collaboration and interaction. They work well with others and are natural leaders. Games give these students a way to socialize, yet still remain on task with their learning goals. Games also provide an opportunity for these students to test out their leadership skills in a safe environment.

HOW GAMES BRING LEARNING TO YOUR CLASSROOM

Games deliver a welcome variation to the tell-and-test classroom format. The games in this book will make your lessons more enticing and motivate your students to learn more and, more important, *enjoy* learning more. These games can be adapted very easily to most themes and subjects that your school's curriculum has outlined. As an educator, you have goals for yourself, to tap into each child's *zone* where he gets excited about learning and has continued moments of success that drive him to undertake further challenges.

Students have goals for themselves, too—they want to succeed, they want to do well in school, and they want to learn the best they can. Games help satisfy everyone's goals. They keep the curriculum fresh and interesting, which is key to motivating future learning.

Here are fourteen ways games bring your curriculum to your audience:

1. *Games are experiential.* Today's student needs to do and to try things on her own. These games bring her into direct contact with the topic; she will actively interact with your information wrapped in a game. Games also allow you to observe her real-time behavior.

2. *Games allow special tutoring for one or two.* On occasion you need to work with only one or two students. Games can be customized with almost any topic and used in the home or classroom for special tutoring sessions. You will find additional tips on how to use each game in this book in the "Teacher's Notes" and "Customizing" sections.

3. *Games provide choices for your classroom.* Educators sometimes feel weighed down by assigned curricula and audiences. Games allow you to add variety and flexibility to your teaching menus. Here is a brief list of your classroom choices with games:

   - In-chair or out-of-chair play

   - Table, floor, or wall play

   - In-class or learning center activities

   - Small- or large-group play

   - Teacher or student scoring

   - In-class or take-home assignments

   - Individual or team play

   - Introduction or review of material

   - Open-book or closed-book play

   - Inside or outside play

4. *Games reinforce learning.* Games give you playful ways to present and represent material to your students. During this play, your students can practice and demonstrate what they have learned from lecture and readings.

5. *Games provide immediate feedback.* Students want and need feedback on their performance. Games give students immediate feedback on the quality of their input—with appropriate corrective feedback. This can become an invaluable learning opportunity.

6. *Games improve test-taking skills.* Because of the playful challenge inherent in them, games serve as excellent practice for test taking. They expose students to a variety of question areas and formats, and postgame discussion can focus on test-taking tips from both the teacher and fellow students.

7. *Game playing shows that classroom energy is good.* Sometimes the educator has to deal with the energy that children bring into the classroom. Using games reinforces the concept that energy is a good thing and that the classroom is a good place to expend energy. In addition, games can bring students' focus back to the curriculum following active play periods such as recess.

8. *Games can introduce new or difficult material.* Games have an unparalleled facility to introduce new or difficult material to willing participants. Because the game format is playful, the inherent challenge of new or difficult material is much less threatening than it is ordinarily. During game play the seeming unsolvable question is "just part of the game." And educators can use the window following a correct response to successfully introduce new information. One method, for example, is to give an in-class assignment on a new reading. After ten minutes of individual work, bring students into small groups to share their understanding of the material.

9. *Games complement reading assignments.* Games work very well to complement in-class or at-home reading. Use game sheets as homework guides or use in-class question-and-answer sheets.

10. *Games improve teamwork.* Because games are real-time activities that bring students into teams, they train students in the rules of working together as a team and underscore the value of team collaboration.

11. *Games teach playing within the rules.* Games continually reinforce the concept that the only way to win is to play within the rules. If an instance of "fair play" or "cheating" is aired, the postgame discussion can deal with issues of cooperation and honesty.

12. *Games foster both individual and team achievement.* Games underscore the importance of both the individual and the team by giving the student a chance to work alone and then adding the dimension of bringing him into a small group to share ideas.

13. *Games reinforce and improve multitasking.* Games allow students, individually or in groups, to experience and practice multiskill tasks, such as bouncing a balloon while responding to a series of questions. The pressure created by game play helps build problem-solving skills and promotes creativity.

14. *Games can replace drill work.* Games can replace the dreaded memorization work required in learning multiplication tables, spelling, and the like. The required repetition can be carried out in a game format. When the students' attention is focused on the play of the game, memorization becomes less of a chore.

FINAL THOUGHTS

Learning games put an end to the myth that the school curriculum has to be content heavy and offer little engagement. Games provide an experiential learning platform that engages the student while delivering content. Games differ from tell-and-test formats because they provide a vehicle that makes every student a willing player and then they involve the student with the content. Even better, games provide real-time experiences that appeal to auditory, visual, and kinesthetic learners. These experiences can be observed and gently measured to ensure that student comprehension meets educators' goals and expectations.

We hope that you now view games as a way to enhance your curriculum. We now invite you to move to the next chapter to learn more about how to select, develop, and set up your own classroom games.

CHAPTER **TWO**

Selecting an Appropriate Game

Come play my classroom game
And see with smiling eyes
The race that is more fun
Than winning or a prize

—Steve Sugar

The next three chapters are designed to assist you to select and customize *any* game—from this book or from your own library—with your own material. Use these chapters as a guide to and reminder of the steps you must consider in the setup, play, and closure of your own classroom game. After conducting the game, take notes on what worked well and what needed improvement; this information will guide your next use of this kind of learning experience.

Remember, these are your learning games, and they need your customizing in both content and implementation to meet your specific needs in terms of the age, size, and level of your audience.

Consider the following information when selecting a game for your learners.

TARGET AUDIENCE

One of the most important considerations is your target audience. Your game must reflect their knowledge, skills, and abilities.

Games can evoke powerful learning. It begins when the student, now a player, is challenged with the information that provokes a search for the answer. When the correct answer is aired, the learning is immediately reinforced. This learning transfer happens over and over during the game. This *moment of learning* is not only powerful but often remains long after the learning event or game has been completed. Three dimensions of your target audience are level of play, number of players, and class size.

Level of Play

As you would expect, game play varies with the age of the audience in terms of the challenge of the material, the complexity of the rules, and the time of play. To assist you in sorting the games for your needs and audience, we have divided the potential audience into three groups with some distinct needs: grades K–2, grades 3–6, and grades 7–8.

- *Grades K–2.* Learning games for this group should focus on behavioral as well as intellectual skills. Children at this age may still be in the egocentric stage and are just beginning to be introduced to group play. This may make group work a challenge for the young student. Children will learn what games and group play mean overall—that games have winners, contain an element of challenge, and encourage competition. Using teams of fewer than five and simple concepts at the outset of game play allow children to focus on the rules of play. As the concept of a learning game is understood, you can build in additional task complexity.

- *Grades 3–6.* The focus for this audience continues to be how to work cooperatively in groups, but you can also put more emphasis on course curriculum. With students of this age it is developmentally appropriate to move them into larger teams. At this age students will also become very familiar with the concept of testing. Teachers can use games to teach their students about the content and the format of a test—easing their students into formal testing in a friendly environment.

- *Grades 7–8.* Learning games for this group can be expanded to familiarize students with written testing procedures, oral and written directions, forming and working in teams, individual and group problem-solving skills, and individual critical thinking skills.

Number of Players

When games are used in the classroom, any number can play. Although many games seem best suited for a small number of players, the intrigue and challenge of play invites the involvement of larger groups of participants. Interaction with the play of the game is vital because it brings your students into active contact with the topic.

Participation in a team is an important element of the game experience—it immerses students in a collaborative learning environment. Teams not only present a collective approach to problem solving but also reduce the threat students might feel during a question-and-response period. If an individual responds incorrectly, she may feel embarrassed or unprepared. If the team responds incorrectly, team members have a mixed experience of both disappointment and discovery. Working in teams also shows players that all learning does not have to come from the teacher.

The size of a good working team varies from two to seven players. Teams usually function better with an odd number of players, such as three, five, or seven. Try to use three-member teams unless the game rules indicate otherwise. Using three players allows all players to get involved in the responses and other aspects of game play.

The size of your class requires you to vary the focus of your control. In smaller groups you will be able to reinforce the topic during presentation of the question-and-response material. The natural energies and distractions of larger classes require more maintenance and direct control.

- *Group size of 1 to 2.* This *very small* group requires one-on-one skills from the educator and a game format that can be adapted to one-on-one play. The contest pits the player or players against a preset time or score. Feedback can be tailored to the student— either in the form of an immediate score or as a mix of score and tutoring.

- *Group size of 3 to 14.* This *small* group allows a casual game atmosphere in which the teacher and students participate at a high level. In a small group there is time to go over each question, reach in-depth closure, and ensure each child understands the material. For a group of three to five players, consider having the students run the group, using the game as a learning center activity.

- *Group size of 15 to 25.* A *medium* group requires greater class management skills. The teacher must decide whether she will run one game for the entire class or break the class into teams for whole-group games—perhaps two to four games for this medium class size. Conducting multiple games requires you to make preparations for the additional activity, disruption, and noise.

- *Group size of 26 to 46.* A *large* group presents class management problems that require the teacher to decide whether he needs personnel assistance (other classroom monitors) and to plan room logistics that accommodate all the players. One method might be to divide the students into two sets and run the games in two rounds—in the first round one set of students acts as players and the second set acts as observers, and in the second round the roles are reversed. Again, remember that conducting multiple games requires you to make preparations for the additional activity, disruption, and noise.

LEARNING OUTCOMES

Games can reinforce many different behavioral and learning outcomes. Your learning outcome can vary from the reinforcement of the topic to the demonstration of how to participate in a working group. It is important to establish a set of learning objectives—what you want the participants to learn or demonstrate during and after playing the game. Then you can evaluate how the game met your expectations.

Games are excellent vehicles for learners to demonstrate the following skills and abilities, all within the friendly and competitive game environment:

- Understanding of the concepts of rules, cooperative play, and winning and losing.

- Understanding of the classroom material.

- Application of concepts and principles found in the classroom material.

- Problem solving and strategizing.

PLAYING TIME

Time of play is always a critical issue. Game play represents only part of the total classroom time required. The total learning experience is a three-part process of setup, game play, and closure.

- *Setup time: approximately 20 percent of total.* During this time, you establish the game environment by preparing the room, distributing game materials, dividing learners into teams, and reviewing the rules of play.

- *Game playing time: approximately 60 percent of total.* This is the actual playing of the game, including the start and stop of game play, clarifying questions about rules or content, validation and elaboration of correct responses, and declaring winners.

- *Closure time: approximately 20 percent of total.* This portion of the time is for processing game content and player conduct. During this time the teacher brings the class "back to the classroom" and revisits the learning concepts covered during game play.

Teachers must plan for a *total* learning experience, considering several factors including the complexity of the topic, time required for setup and closure, time of day, and even the attention span of the participants. Because of these factors, all the games in this book are designed to be played in fifty minutes or less. Of course, if you find that a game generates a highly motivating environment, you may extend the time of play by conducting additional rounds or adding supplemental questions or tasks.

THE WHOLE COURSE GAME

When a particular game proves both popular and effective, consider reusing it as appropriate throughout the entire school semester or year. This *whole course* technique allows you to reintroduce a game experience that is familiar to both student and teacher. Advantages of a whole course game are

- Immediate acceptance of a game format that has already proven successful in reinforcing learning or behavior outcomes.

- Familiarity with the rules and roles involved in game play.

- Immediate focus on content in the form of game questions and situations.

- Readily available game accessories from previous play and easier setup for game play.

- Ease of updating to match your current curriculum requirements.

GAME VARIATIONS

Once you have selected a game and played it with your students, you may want to modify one or more of these game format elements to meet your classroom needs.

- *Class size.* Most games in this book are designed to accommodate four to twelve players. Modifications should be made to accommodate groups larger than twelve or to simplify rules and question material to play with one or two players.

  1–2 players. The teacher directly participates in the administration and scoring of the game. Revise the competition process by substituting standard scores or times in place of other teams' performance.

  3–14 players. Little or no modification is needed for this small group.

  15–25 players. Modify for medium groups by allowing more time for game play, preparing additional materials, and revisiting your logistics to make sure your classroom can accommodate the requirements of the game.

  26–46 players. Major modifications are required for large groups to ensure that players understand and follow the rules and that the dynamics of game play do not overwhelm the playing area. Many teachers have found that using one or two assistants—especially in the first run of the game—helps with crowd control and speeds up setup and closure.

- *Time of play.* Expand or contract the total time allowed for the entire game depending on the number of rounds or questions or the amount of material you wish to cover in the time allowed. The rule of thumb is to expand the playing time for groups over fifteen; expand topic coverage for groups under five.

- *Focus of the task.* Adjust the levels of competition and cooperation or encourage extra teamwork or creativity, and the like.

  Grades K–2. The focus should be on the manner of play, such as following the rules and demonstrating appropriate behavior, as well as on providing the correct responses. The concepts of winning and losing are introduced at this level.

  Grades 3–6. Students should understand how to play games. The focus is on demonstrating an understanding of the topic as well as on demonstrating appropriate game and social behavior including sportsmanship—how to be a *good winner* as well as a *good loser.*

  Grades 7–8. In addition to answering questions on the topic, students can be challenged with problem-solving and critical thinking tasks. The teacher may ask for greater student involvement in conducting and observing the game and even in writing questions for the game.

- *Scoring procedure.* Revise rewards and penalties as necessary.

These elements are a starting point for modifying games to suit your particular educational purpose. Each of the game descriptions in this book provides further, specific recommendations for adjustments to the four elements of class size, time of play, focus of the task, and scoring procedure.

FINAL THOUGHTS

Choosing the right game for your classroom is an important first step toward a successful game experience. We now invite you to review guidelines for *loading your game,* that is, placing your content into the game format. We have found that most teachers are familiar with many of these guidelines but appreciate the step-by-step process as a reminder.

CHAPTER THREE

Developing Game Content

The biggest contributing factor to a game's success
is what the teacher does to prepare the game
for classroom play.

—Karen Lawson, *The Trainer's Handbook*

The content material—in the form of questions and situations—is the "heart" of the game. If the selected game format is successful in driving students' interest in the content, then it is up to the quality of the questions to deliver the learning experience.

DESIRED OBJECTIVES

Review your learning objectives. What do you want the students to learn from the game play? The games in this book are best suited for the review of information by recounting specific data and identifying required items.

LOADING YOUR GAME

Loading, or placing your content into the game, is a threefold process of selection, translation, and incorporation.

1. Select suitable information items to present during game play. These items, usually found in your lesson plan, lecture, and readings, can be featured as individual points of learning.

2. Translate these items into game-sized information nuggets. Turn them into short questions, mini-case studies, or situations. As you write out each question or situation, also note the preferred response, the rationale for that response (for elaboration during the answer period), and the reference source (for your own documentation and use).

3. Incorporate the questions or situations into the game format by transferring them to individual question cards or multiple-item question sheets. Many teachers find that noting the topic, lesson, and date on the question sheets reminds them how these questions were used and assists them in updating the material when they use the game again later.

The following loading techniques are helpful in selecting and translating material for the game format. You can use them individually or in a mix.

The Review Test

This is the most popular loading technique among teachers. It has three steps:

1. Develop thirty to fifty test items that embody the most important concepts and facts of the lesson module.

2. Place the items in an order that creates a conceptual flow. Some teachers, however, prefer to use a random sequence of items to represent the "luck of the draw" more typical of game play.

3. Assign values to the questions as necessary. Assigning additional points to an important fact or concept underscores its importance in your curriculum.

Information Triage

When using this loading technique, you review your topic information and highlight important items and facts. Revisit your information, and sort the material into *keep* and *drop* categories. Repeat the process until you have thirty to fifty items. Revisit your items and place them in an order that creates a conceptual (or random) flow. Assign values to the questions as necessary.

Zoom In-Zoom Out

Remove yourself, or *zoom out,* from your material to gain a holistic overview. What is it that you want your students to demonstrate during the course of a game? Then *zoom in* on specific situations or questions that illustrate your learning points. Continue this technique until you generate a tapestry of learning items that reinforce and assess the students' understanding of learning concepts. Place the items in an order that creates a conceptual (or random) flow, and assign values to the questions as necessary.

WRITING QUESTIONS

Appropriately written questions add to both the learning and fun of the game. Old tests are helpful when writing questions, as are the test banks that accompany classroom texts. Another question development strategy is to ask the older students to write questions for the game. Teachers have found that student-developed questions not only add to the question bank but also provide two important student insights into the material—what the students feel is important and what the students do not understand.

Here are some reminders for developing information items for your classroom game.

- Write questions in a conversational tone. Because game questions are usually read aloud, this helps the flow of the game.

- Write closed-ended questions, questions that focus on one response. This ensures that the requested information and its rationale are covered in the question-and-response format.

- Focus each question on one fact. This keeps the information precise and brief. If needed, use several questions to ensure that a concept is covered adequately.

- Be brief. Use simple wording for questions and encourage brief answers. As a rule, questions should contain less than thirty-five words.

- Take advantage of the moment of learning that follows a correct answer. After the correct response is presented, players are usually curious about why this answer is the correct response, so give them the rationale for the answer at this time. This immediate feedback is a feature of a good learning experience.

- Develop a review question to preview question mix of three to one. A game is an excellent vehicle for presenting new material. Question material new to the audience can be considered part of the randomness of play. The rule of thumb is to create three questions that review material already covered for every one question that previews upcoming material. This not only creates a good question mix but also piques interest in new topics.

- Mix the difficulty. Try for a correct response rate of 50 percent by creating a question difficulty mix of one-three-one—one challenging question, three moderate questions, and one easy question. Introduce the game with the easy and moderate questions to help new players feel comfortable with the game play and content. As players become more comfortable with the rules and roles of the game, they can focus on more challenging questions.

- Number each question. This helps you with your question count and gives you a way to quickly identify and review questions that may require adjustment, deletion, or updating.

Sample Question Formats

Teachers are very proficient question writers; it is our way to challenge, test, and review information. Our question-writing skill makes us natural development resources for any classroom game. The following list of sample question formats is meant to be a reminder and a guide to you about the different ways you can deliver your content wrapped in a game format.

Note that it is very important that you state or restate the complete response when you validate a correct response. This reinforcement encourages greater understanding, internalization, and application of the information.

- *Direct.* This type of question requires players to identify a person, place, or thing. Be sure to include enough information in the question that players can provide the proper answer.

  Q: Name one of the three primary colors.

  A: Accept any one of the following: red, yellow, or blue. (If the student responds, "blue," verify the correctness of the response and then elaborate on it: "Blue is one of the three primary colors. The other two primary colors are red and yellow.")

- *Fill-in-the-blank.* This question requires the player to supply the information required by a blank space. This format is a little simpler than the direct question because you specify more precisely what is expected in the blank space.

  Q: The three primary colors are red, yellow, and _____.

  A: Blue. (Restate: "The three primary colors are red, yellow, and blue.")

- *Multiple choice.* This format presents the correct response along with two distracting responses. This format can make a difficult item easier because it presents a limited choice of answers to the player. Questions should focus on no more than three choices; four (or more) choices can be confusing and slow down play.

  Q: Which of the following is *not* one of the three primary colors?

      a. Red

      b. Yellow

      c. Green

  A: Green. (The other primary color is blue. Restate: "The three primary colors are red, yellow, and blue.")

- *True or false.* This is the easiest kind of question to prepare and answer, and it offers players a fifty-fifty chance to respond correctly. It can help players ease into competition. Limit this question format to fewer than 25 percent of all the game questions, however, to keep the game from becoming a flip-of-the-coin match.

  Q: The three primary colors are red, green, and yellow. True or false?

  A: False. (Green is not a primary color. Restate: "The three primary colors are red, yellow, and blue.")

- *Partial listing.* This question format requires the identification of multiple items in a category or listing. Ask for some but not all of the items. That way you can underscore the importance of the complete list without frustrating players by asking them to recall the complete list. Read the total list when the answer is given.

  Q: Name two of the three primary colors.

  A: Accept any two of the three: red, yellow, and blue. (Restate: "The three primary colors are red, yellow, and blue.")

- *Demonstration*. This format requires the player to perform a particular skill or task.

    Q: Using any or all of the primary colors on the palette, create the color green.

    A: The player mixes blue and yellow to get green. The teacher can validate the color and then compare it to a color on a prepared palette. The teacher may wish to demonstrate a variety of ways to mix and use colors on the palette.

LESSON MATERIAL

The use of a learning game can introduce the student to a topic or concept, demonstrate how much the student understands about that topic, underscore appropriate behavioral traits, or simply encourage further interest in classroom proceedings. You may wish to develop appropriate lesson materials to elaborate your topic in the context of the game, such as an introductory or closing lecture, visual charts or posters, models, a hands-on demonstration, or supplemental readings.

Using a variety of media can also add to the total learning experience. Consider such media as music, videotapes, posters, newspaper or magazine articles, models, Internet materials or Web pages, and in-class demonstrations.

Games Used to Reinforce Readings

For older students, develop a handout that is more than just take-home information from the presentation and that contains ideas and resources for both student and parent. If such handouts or homework assignments are distributed before the game, game play will then reward those students who preread the assigned material. Games have been known to encourage the completion of out-of-class assignments—no player likes to let her team down during game play.

Game Sheets Used as Homework

Another way to encourage at-home learning is to create a *working* handout by adapting a game sheet from one of this book's games, such as Dilemma, Guggenheim, or Scavenger Hunt. Working from the reading assignment, students develop as many responses as possible. The next day students reinforce this assignment by participating in ongoing work groups to share and compare their game sheet responses. This is a very powerful strategy because, once again, students do not want to let down the rest of their team.

Classroom Reading Used as an Instant Game

Many teachers have found that using a game instantly turns an ordinary classroom reading into an event. First, hand out the reading to your students and give them five to ten minutes to read over the material. Then form the students into groups and conduct a quiz in the form of a game. This will underscore the material and bring renewed interest to future classroom readings.

FINAL THOUGHTS

This chapter has introduced the basics for developing your game content. Even though each classroom game introduces some additional work in the areas of development, setup, and play, you will find that the payoff—in terms of student engagement and learning—makes the extra effort well worth it. And of course, each game will be easier to develop and play in the future.

This book also offers the following two resources to help you use games in response to classroom challenges:

- Appendix Two: Sample Game Lessons. This appendix presents two topic- and grade-related challenges and a game plan that walks you through the preparation of a game that specifically meets each challenge.

- Appendix Three: Games for Special Situations. This appendix suggests games you can use to deal with five classroom challenges—the first week, test preparation, material review, active days, and learning centers.

In the next chapter we discuss the physical and mental preparations needed to set up and conduct a classroom game.

CHAPTER FOUR

Setting Up and Running a Game

Be flexible. Although games and activities have rules, don't become obsessed with them. An important requirement for an effective game experience is to maintain your sense of humor and to take serious things playfully.

—Sivasailam Thiagarajan and Glenn Parker,
Teamwork and Team Play

This chapter focuses on the physical and mental preparation needed to set up and conduct a classroom game. It covers assembling the game accessories, the pregame setup, game play, and closure.

GAME ACCESSORIES

Game accessories are materials, equipment, or props that create an appropriate learning game environment. Here are some reminder lists, along with hints on using these accessories during a game.

Audiovisual Equipment

- *Chalkboard.* This standard of the classroom can be used to reinforce key lecture points, display rules of play, state appropriate behavior during game play, keep score, list questions or discussion items, note problems with a game or game equipment, or list comments to be covered during the debriefing. You may also post items on the chalkboard such as posters or newsprint lists of the rules of play or theme charts.

- *Overhead projector.* Overhead slides can be used to reinforce a lecture, display a game format and rules of play, keep score, list key elements of discussion, or list comments and reactions. This tool is especially helpful with large groups. Some teachers even display the game sheet on an overhead to establish the rules and dynamics of game play.

- *Cassette or CD player.* An audio player can be used to provide audio commentary, stories, sing-along choruses, background music, and random times for rounds of play.

Materials

- *Masking tape.* Use masking tape to place charts and posters on walls, place cards on wall charts, mend paper items, secure electrical wires to the floor or wall, and so on.

- *Posters or charts.* Commercial posters or personally developed charts can be used to reinforce the learning and to create a playful game environment. *Theme charts* can underscore concepts from the curriculum or current events or model behavioral expectations.

- *Bulletin boards.* Use bulletin boards to post rules of play or to present "best scores" and other information. Some teachers select a special board both to display game rules and to keep game supplies handy in pockets made from cardboard, envelopes, or library cardholders. You can dedicate the board to a unit of study, encouraging students to refer to the information posted on the board during the game.

- *Newsprint easels.* Newsprint can be used to post directions or to record comments and observations made during the run of the game.

  Note: Rules of play and other lists and charts can be taken down and stored for future use. This not only models the recycling of class materials but shortens the setup time for future play. It even allows the teacher to introduce a game at a moment's notice.

- *Whiteboard (dry-erase board).* This alternative to the chalkboard can also be used to hang posters or charts. Some teachers may want to create a game board using the whiteboard, attaching sticky magnets to the back of item cards or other game props.

Special Props

- *Timer.* Use a stopwatch or kitchen timer to time rounds, the entire play of the game, or question-and-answer periods.

- *Noisemaker.* The natural energy of game play can drown out even the most vigorous voice. An alternate way of getting attention can add to the playful game environment as well as save your voice. The noisemaker can alert players when to start, stop, offer a correct response, return from a break, and so on. Some commonly found noisemakers are call bells (think of room service at a hotel), chimes, dinner bells, whistles, train whistles, and kazoos.

- *Name cards.* Use these cards to bolster team identities or to identify processes of the game, such as the special tasks in Medley Relay. You can make these cards by folding five-by-eight-inch cover stock in half.

- *Question and direction cards.* A set of question cards that students can draw from is used in teacher-controlled games and card games. However, many teachers have found that printing out question cards is time consuming and that due to changes in curriculum the cards are short-lived. The preferred way to use these small cards is for giving specific directions, such as "Stop Play," or for assigning point values to questions read from a prepared list.

- *Raffle tickets.* Use these tickets for prize drawings during or after game play. Tickets can be created from portions of three-by-five-inch index cards or purchased in rolls from teacher supply catalogues and stores. Some teachers like to collect a raffle ticket from everyone in the class at the beginning of the period. Then winning players and teams get to put in additional tickets. This gives everyone a chance to win the drawing for the prize, with the game winners receiving a slight edge.

- *Miscellaneous containers.* Depending on the requirements of the game, the containers needed can range from bowls to paper bags to trash cans to egg cartons to milk cartons. In Grab Bag a paper bag makes an excellent container for the prize tickets. In Trash Ball an ordinary trash can serves as a basketball receptacle. In Medley Relay gallon milk and empty egg containers are used as objects passed around a player circle in a relay-style race.

- *Miscellaneous items.* Sometimes a game may require miscellaneous items such as balloons, milk cartons, game sheet markers, bubble makers, and so forth. The criteria for any item to be used in a game for children are availability, convenience (easy to find and store), cost effectiveness, familiarity to the player, and safety, especially when used in the presence of younger children.

- *Markers.* Some games require a marker to temporarily cover a space or to indicate status on a game sheet. Traditionally, markers are pawns or chips. But almost anything can be used as a marker, such as pieces of felt, bits of construction paper, pebbles, pennies or other coins, paper clips, buttons, Magic Marker tops, and so forth.

- *Pass, juggle, or throw items.* These items vary from crumpled paper, used in Trash Ball, to balloons, used in Balloon Juggle, to odd-sized containers, used in Medley Relay. These items must be safe, easy to locate, and cost effective.

  Note: Use caution when introducing balloons. Be careful that children, especially the younger set, do not bite the balloons or poke objects into them. A bursting balloon can cause problems, especially when near the nose and mouth of a child.

- *Bubble makers.* In the game Bubbles, these simple devices introduce the wonder of bubbles as part of a learning experience. The teacher may want to keep the bubbles confined to a specific area with a ready supply of wipe-up cloths or have the students play the game on a specially prepared area, such as a spread-out drop cloth.

GAME SETUP

Setup time is the critical period for readying the classroom and yourself—especially for the first playing of the game. Take this time to mentally and physically revisit your play area as you walk through your game. Conduct an inspection of the room, checking for any hazards to safety or obstacles that will inhibit play. Set up or move tables and chairs, as required. Place posters, banners, worksheets, or wall charts containing suitable quotations or artwork. Later, post rules of play or other materials as required.

After you feel satisfied with the safety and logistics of the room, take on the perspective of your students as you enter the room. Is the room visually attractive? Does it anticipate a joyful game experience?

Set aside one table or area as *your* resource area. Take time to organize this table or area with the game sheets and accessories so you will have easy access to them during game play.

- Lay out additional reference materials as required.

- Lay out game sheets and score sheets for distribution before and during the games.

- Lay out the necessary accessories—such as noisemakers, masking tape, question cards, markers, and prizes.

Take this time to ensure that the equipment and materials are appropriate and prepared. For example, attend to these items:

- *Chalkboard.* Make sure that the chalkboard is clean and that you have sufficient white and colored chalk.

- *Whiteboard.* Make sure that the board is clean and that you have sufficient water-soluble markers and erasers. Some teachers find it helpful to keep a bottle of a cleaner with ammonia available to clean the board in emergencies.

- *Overhead projector.* Make sure the projector is operable, is focused, has an electric cord sufficiently long and secured to the floor, is placed on a workable stand, and has an extra bulb.

- *Easel and newsprint.* Make sure you have markers and enough sheets of paper to display the rules, record student comments, or present additional information.

- *Tables and chairs.* Take this time to set up or remove tables and chairs as required.

PRELIMINARIES

These *preliminaries* are the in-class procedures prior to actual game play that help create the structure for the game and a game play environment. They may include these activities:

- Dividing the class into subgroups or teams.

- Seating each team at its own table.

- Getting players lined up in established game play areas.

- Having teams select team names.

- Getting teams to assign roles to players and establishing procedures for knowing which team member should respond to a question.

- Distributing game materials, including game sheets and paper and pencils.

- Distributing score sheets, question or problem sheets, and other game materials and props.

- Displaying game information and player instructions.

Next, introduce the game to the students, describing the rules. This introduction, along with an interesting classroom layout, should help motivate your students to play. Students often reflect and take on the enthusiasm displayed by the teacher.

The teacher may also want to ask if there are any questions about the rules. The teacher may also ask one or more students to restate the rules to ensure that the players understand what is expected of them.

Here is a sample introduction for the game Alphabet Soup.

> Good morning, I want to briefly go over the game Alphabet Soup. The game objective is to score the most points by putting together the letter cards assigned to your team. The game is played in rounds. Each round consists of a team getting five letter cards and then putting together as many words using these cards as the team members can in the time allowed. When time is called, each team is awarded points for each word. After each team has played an equal number of rounds, the team with the most points wins.

GAME PLAY

Games are played as described in detail in Part Two. Here is an example, drawing once again on Alphabet Soup.

Round 1. The first team to play, "Team A," assigns the roles of the *letter carriers*—those players who will each hold a letter card—and the "recorder"—the player who writes down each formed word. After the teacher is assured that Team A members understand their assignments, she begins the game. Team A begins forming its first word with the letter cards. The players holding the letter cards arrange themselves in the order of the first word—the first player showing "c," the second player showing "a," the third player showing "r," and the fourth player showing "s" to form the four-letter word *cars*. As soon as the recorder writes down this word, the team forms another word. This continues until the three-minute period is over. The teacher collects Team A's list from the recorder.

After receiving Team A's list the teacher should write each word on the chalkboard and elaborate on its validity and value. As with any game situation, expect periodic resistance, defensiveness, or conflict during game play. Remember that even though there may be designated correct and incorrect responses, participants may have other perspectives on what answers are right and what answers are wrong. The disclosure of the correct words is an important moment of learning in which the energy of the game drives students to discover not only *what* was correct but also *why* your selected response is the most appropriate response. The teacher's role is not simply to impose a correct answer but to get the students to sort out their assumptions, and to encourage them to think about the information and concepts presented by the game.

The game is played the same way for all rounds. After each team has played an equal number of rounds, the teacher tallies the point totals and declares one team the winner.

GAME CLOSURE

In the afterglow of the game, students' attention can be refocused on the topic and on any problems the players encountered during game play, such as confusion about the rules or roles, time periods, or even the quality of the questions or the responses.

Competitive Feelings

In the event of very competitive play, you may have to allow your students time to cool down, and you may have to encourage appropriate behavior by both the winners and the losers. This is the time for your players to transform back into students and to transfer positive learning experiences from the game back to the classroom. You may have to remind your players that the goal was not just to win or get the right answers but also to show that they understood the topic. Also remind your players that all competitive feelings, if any, should stay in the room. For example, one teacher, sensing that too many competitive feelings lingered after a game, selected a nearby trash can and designated it as the receptor of all competitive feelings. After all feelings were "sent" to the trash can, she had the can moved to a "safe" place, and she and the students returned to the after-game discussion.

Reflection

Closure can be extended to the process of helping students to reflect on their experiences in order to develop meaningful learning. Reflection usually takes place immediately after the game experience. This period can include venting, in which students let off steam, their feelings about specific things; making applications of the game and its content to classroom learning; and offering generalizations, such as comments that relate game play and content to real-life behavior.

Journal Writing

Older students can write down their reactions, learned concepts, and observed behavior in a journal. This reinforces writing skills and allows the teacher to revisit the game through the eyes of the student. Where group discussion is limited, a journal allows students to share what they have learned and raise questions about the lesson or game in a one-on-one discussion with the teacher.

This period of the game can also be used to do any or all of the following:

- Shift the focus from the game back to the classroom.

- Thank students for their participation and contributions to the success of the game.

- Congratulate the winners or all players on the successful completion of the game.

- Have players congratulate each other for achievements made during the game.

- Tie up loose ends of the game, and resolve any confusion about the rules or questions covered during the game.

- Review and share observations about the game and game play.

- Relate what was learned from the game material and from game play to the classroom topic or overall concepts of the material.

- Distribute certificates or awards.

- Discuss any new information or concepts raised during the game.

FINAL THOUGHTS

Teaching through a game offers you a unique opportunity to match the personality of the game—its ability to evoke playfulness and energy—to the demands of the curriculum and your students. No matter how many times you play the same game, even with the same material and participants, reactions will differ. Each group of students has its own learning thresholds and perceptions of what is new and important. One of your rewards is to experience the joy of discovery along with each set of players.

Remember also that these games can be either used as stand-alone activities—to introduce, teach, review, or test learning—or sequenced with other activities to create a specific learning mix.

Finally, each game description in the following pages offers sample play along with tips on customizing the game for your audience. This should help you select and adapt material for the critical first rounds of play. Then, as you feel more comfortable with the game, you can customize game play further by varying the topics and rules. In addition, be sure to refer to Appendixes One through Four for additional information on selecting and adapting games.

Now we invite you to use these games creatively in your own class-room.

Let the games begin . . .

PART TWO

TWENTY-FIVE GAMES

Activity Cards

INTRODUCTION

Activity cards is a fast-moving game played by two or more teams. A game card designates the point value of each upcoming question. When players answer correctly, they collect the stated number of points. A team's turn ends when its time expires or a "Stop Play" card is drawn. The game has an exciting element of randomness, and the contents of the activity cards can be customized in many ways to students' needs.

| **Purpose** | • To experience direct involvement in the subject matter. |
| | • To increase understanding and ability to apply information. |

| **Game Objective** | To collect the most points after two or more rounds of play. |

| **Players** | 4 or more. *Can be adapted for one-to-one tutoring.* |

| **Time** | 15–45 minutes. |

| **Grades** | 3–8. |

Supplies	• 1 set of activity cards printed with point values or directions.
	• 1 set of questions prepared in advance by the teacher.
	• Chalkboard with scoring columns for each team.
	• 1-minute timer or stopwatch.

GAME STEPS

Preliminaries	• Divide class into two or three teams.
	• Shuffle the activity deck and place the cards face down on the instructor's table.
	• Inform teams they have sixty seconds to respond correctly to as many questions as they can.

Round 1: Team A	• Select the first activity card, and read it aloud.
	• Read the first question from the prepared list of questions. (Players from Team A may meet briefly before responding to a question.)
	• First team responds.

Scoring	A *correct* response = number of points shown on card

An *incorrect* response = 0 points

- Have team continue to play until a "Stop Play" card is drawn or time expires.

- Tally Team A's points, and post them on the chalkboard.

Round 2 to End of Game

Play continues in this fashion until all teams have completed an equal number of rounds.

End of Game The team with the most points is declared the winner.

SCORING EXAMPLE

Preliminaries

- The class is divided into three teams: Team A, Team B, and Team C.

- Each group meets at one of the tables.

Round 1: Team A

Question = 1 point

- The teacher shuffles the activity deck and places the cards face down.

- The teacher starts the 1-minute timer.

- The teacher selects and shows the *first* activity card: *Question is worth 1 point.*

- The teacher presents the first question from the set of questions.

- Players from Team A confer and then present a response.

- Team A responds correctly. Team A earns 1 point.

- The teacher selects and shows the *second* activity card: *Question is worth 1 point.*

- The teacher presents the second question from the set of questions.

- Players confer and respond.

- Team A responds correctly. Team A earns 1 point.

- The teacher selects and shows the *third* activity card: *Question is worth 3 points.*

- The teacher presents the third question. Team A responds correctly.

- Team A earns 3 points.

- The teacher selects and shows the *fourth* activity card: *Stop Play. End of Round!*

- This completes Team A's round of play.

- All points are totaled for Team A.

- Team A = 1 + 1 + 3 = 5 points.

- The teacher posts Team A's score on the chalkboard.

```
Stop Play.

End
of Round!
```

	Team A	
Round 1	5	

Round 1: Team B

- The teacher shuffles the activity deck and places the cards face down.

- The teacher starts the 1-minute timer.

- The teacher selects and shows the *first* activity card: *Question is worth 1 point.*

- The teacher presents the first question.

- Team B responds correctly. Team B earns 1 point.

Double
or
Nothing

- The teacher selects and shows the *second* activity card: *Question is worth 1 point.*

- The teacher presents the second question.

- Team B responds correctly. Team B earns 1 point.

- The teacher selects and shows the *third* activity card: *Double or Nothing.*

- The teacher presents the third question.

- Team B responds incorrectly. Team B loses all of its points.

- Continue playing.

- The teacher selects and shows the *fourth* activity card: *Question is worth 1 point.*

- The teacher presents the fourth question.

- Team B responds correctly. Team B earns 1 point.

- The teacher selects and shows the *fifth* activity card: *Question is worth 3 points.*

- The teacher presents the fifth question.

- Team B responds correctly. Team B earns 3 points.

- Time expires. This completes Team B's round.

- All points are totaled for Team B.

- Team B = $1 + 1 - 2 + 1 + 3 = 4$ points.

- The teacher posts Team B's score on the chalkboard.

	Team A	Team B	
Round 1	5	4	

Round 1: Team C

- The teacher shuffles the activity deck and places the cards face down.

- The teacher starts the one-minute timer.

- The teacher selects and shows the *first* activity card: *Question is worth 3 points.*

- The teacher presents the first question.

- Team C responds incorrectly. Team C earns 0 points.

- The teacher selects and shows the *second* activity card: *Question is worth 1 point.*

- The teacher presents the second question.

- Team C responds correctly. Team C earns 1 point.

- The teacher selects and shows the *third* activity card: *Question is worth 2 points.*

- The teacher presents the third question.

- Team C responds correctly. Team C earns 2 points.

- The teacher selects and shows the *fourth* activity card: *Double or Nothing.*

- The teacher presents the fourth question.

- Team C responds correctly. Team C earns double all points from the first three questions, for a total of $2 \times (0 + 1 + 2) = 6$ points.

- The teacher selects and shows the *fifth* activity card: *Question is worth 3 points.*

- The teacher presents the fifth question.

- Team C responds incorrectly. Team C earns 0 points.

- Time expires. This completes Team C's round.

- All points are totaled for Team C.

- Team C $= 2 \times (0 + 1 + 2) = 6$ points.

- The teacher posts Team C's score on the chalkboard.

Double
or
Nothing

	Team A	Team B	Team C
Round 1	5	4	6

TEACHER NOTES

- At first glance this game may appear complicated. But it is only a two-step process of drawing an activity card—to establish the scoring procedure for the next question—and then presenting the question. Once played, this game will quickly become a classroom favorite for its rapid flow and the dynamics of the scoring.

- Be sure to review *all* responses at the end of each round of play. This is the *moment of learning,* when the students are open to the correct responses and the rationale you give in your elaboration.

- Using an audio player, use the background music that accompanies popular quiz programs, such as *Jeopardy* or *Who Wants to Be a Millionaire.*

- Select a player from each team to act as *recorder.* The teacher informs the recorder of the number of points scored on each question. Then, at the end of the round, the recorder adds up the points and gives the teacher the listing and the total points scored during the round. Using a recorder helps the teacher track the score and also helps the recorder (and observing students from other teams) deal with real-life math skills.

- Prepare a set of sixteen activity cards.

  - Method 1: Create the cards from three-by-five-inch index cards:

    7 cards showing: Question is worth 1 point.

    4 cards showing: Question is worth 2 points.

    2 cards showing: Question is worth 3 points.

    2 cards showing: Stop Play. End of Round!

    1 card showing: Double *or* Nothing. Double or Lose all previously earned points.

- Method 2: Photocopy and cut out the sixteen cards found on the two activity card sheets at the end of this game.

- Once you are familiar with the playing of the game, create your own activity cards with different point values, directions, or rewards. For example, you might create a fun "consequence," such as having the team that misses a question sing a song to the rest of the class.

- Have your students create activities or consequences for the activity cards. Select the most appropriate, and use during play.

- This is an excellent way to involve all the students. This game can be used after an active period, such as recess or lunch.

- Have older students contribute questions for game play. This will involve them in the activity and give them a sense of pride when they see one of their questions used during play. Using student questions gives you an idea of students' perspective on the topic as well as helping you timewise.

- This game lends itself to use with younger students, especially when the questions and answers are given and received orally.

- Use this game to take the tedium out of those necessary but sometimes tiresome topics that require drill work, such as multiplication tables, spelling, state capitals, letters of the alphabet, and Amendments to the Constitution.

CUSTOMIZING ACTIVITY CARDS

Size of Group
- For one player:

  Time Driven

  - Have one player respond to as many questions as he can in a one-minute time period.

Quantity Driven

- Have one player compete against an established standard.

- Have one player establish a *best round* and compete to match or better that round.

- Remove all "Stop Play" cards and have play continue until the player misses a question.

- For larger groups:

  - Split the class into sections. Have one section play a set of game rounds, and have the other section watch. Review the results of the game with the entire class.

  - Conduct several games simultaneously. Using student monitors or teacher assistants, divide the students into two (or more) sets consisting of two teams each. The two teams in each set play the game with each other. Review the results of each question and the game results with the entire class.

Time of Play

- Expand or contract the time of each round by allowing less time for the round or by adding or removing "Stop Play" cards.

- For older groups: Introduce random elements into the timing, ending a round whenever a randomly timed function—such as a song—ends.

Focus of the Task

- Stop play when the team misses its first question.

- Stop play when the team misses its second question.

- Without allowing the players to confer before responding to a question, rotate the questions around the team. Ask the first question of the first team member, the second question of the second team member, and so forth.

- Ask a question that requires several responses—such as naming the original thirteen colonies. Stop the round at the first incorrect response, and then award 1 point for each correct response.

- After completion of the round, allow a nonplaying team to respond to any incorrectly answered questions. If correct, this team can add the points to its tally. If the team is incorrect, deduct the value of the question from its tally.

Scoring

- Change the point value of questions.

- For older groups: Deduct the point value of the question for any incorrect response.

Activity Card Sheet 1

Question is worth 1 point.	Question is worth 1 point.
Question is worth 1 point.	Question is worth 1 point.
Question is worth 1 point.	Question is worth 1 point.
Question is worth 1 point.	**Double or Nothing** Double or Lose all previously earned points.

Activity Card Sheet 2

Question is worth 2 points.	Question is worth 2 points.	Question is worth 2 points.	Question is worth 2 points.
Question is worth 3 points.	Question is worth 3 points.	Stop Play. End of Round!	Stop Play. End of Round!

SCORE SHEET
Activity Cards

Round	Team	Team	Team
1			
2			
3			
4			
5			
Total Points			

Activity Cards

- Your team responds to the first question.

  A *correct* response = number of points shown on card

  An *incorrect* response = 0 points

- Continue to play until time expires *or* a "Stop Play" card is drawn.

- Total all points earned by your team.

- After all rounds have been played, the team with the most points wins.

ALPHABET SOUP

INTRODUCTION   Alphabet Soup appeals to learners of all types: kinesthetic, visual, and auditory, and it brings fun to the often rote tasks of letter recognition and spelling. It can be more or less active, according to your needs. Each team receives five letter cards and uses the cards to form as many words of two or more letters as possible in a set time. The score is determined by the number of letters in each word formed during a round of play. A sample word list is provided.

This game was originally created for elementary school children and then adapted to become the game Buzz Word for the organizational teambuilding book *Games That Teach Teams,* by Steve Sugar and George Takacs. Here we have reclaimed and readapted the game for its intended audience.

Purpose	• To build understanding of word combinations.
	• To develop language and spelling skills.
Game Objective	To score the most points by putting together letter cards to form word combinations.
Players	6 or more. *Can be adapted for one-on-one tutoring.*
Time	15–45 minutes.
Grades	1–7.
Supplies	• Several 5-card sets of letter cards (cards with 1 or more letters).
	• 1 sample list of word combinations to serve as a scoring checklist.
	• Paper and pencils for the participants.

GAME STEPS

Preliminaries	• Divide class into teams of six to eight players each.
	• Have each team meet at its own table.
	• Have Team A select five *letter carriers*—these players will receive one letter card each. During game play the letter carriers arrange their letter cards into as many words as they can.
	• Have Team A select a *recorder*—the recorder writes down each word formed by the letter carriers.

Round 1

- Distribute one set of letter cards to each team.

- Give each team three minutes to form as many words as the team members can.

- Have recorder write down each formed word.

- Call time at the end of three minutes.

- Award the appropriate number of points for each correctly formed word.

Scoring

2-letter words = 3 points each

3-letter words = 7 points each

4-letter words = 15 points each

5-letter words = 25 points each

- Post team's score on the chalkboard.

Round 2 to End of Game

- Each round is played in a similar fashion.

End of Game

- The team with the most points wins.

SCORING EXAMPLE

Letter cards | a | e | g | r | t |

- Team A selects five letter carriers. Each letter carrier receives one letter from the set: a, e, g, r, and t.

- Team A has three minutes to form as many words as it can.

- Team A creates its first word, *gate*. The team recorder writes the word on a piece of paper.

- Team A forms another word, *ate*, and the recorder writes down the second word.

- This process continues until time is called.

- The recorder has written down the following list of words: *gate, gear, rate, rat, eat, eart, ate, at, art,* and *great*.

- The teacher reviews the team's list and allows all the words with the exception of *eart*. The teacher awards the following points:

1 @ 5 letters *(great)*	= 1 × 25 =	25 points
3 @ 4 letters *(gate, gear, rate)*	= 3 × 15 =	45 points
4 @ 3 letters *(art, ate, eat, rat)*	= 4 × 7 =	28 points
1 @ 2 letters *(at)*	= 1 × 3 =	3 points
Team Total		*101 points*

- The teacher lists the round 1 score of 101 points on the chalkboard.

TEACHER NOTES

- View this game as creating another avenue for approaching children who have a hard time with traditional spelling study tasks. Alphabet Soup appeals to learners with different learning styles—the kinesthetic learner can touch and handle the letters, the visual learner can see the letters actually combine into words, and the auditory learner can be reinforced by the sounds of the words as they are spoken.

- Use this game in a home-schooling situation by having one child spell words with the cards in a given amount of time. If your student thrives on competition, give him personal goals, such as forming ten words or scoring more than 70 points in three minutes.

- Create a worksheet with letters printed at the top. Have players create as many words as they can from the letters. This can be used as a take-home assignment or learning center activity.

- Create several sets of individual cards for students to use in a learning center activity. This makes the game more hands-on for one or more players—they can actually manipulate and hold the cards in their hands.

- Use *double-letter* cards to match your curriculum needs:

  - Create double-vowel letter card (vowel digraphs) such as *ea*—to reinforce words such as *seat, beat, heat*.

  - Create double-vowel letter cards—such as *oo* or *ee*—to reinforce word such as *foot, feet, boot, beet*.

  - Use a card to represent letter combinations such as *at*—to reinforce words such as *bat, cat, sat, rat, fat*, and the like.

  - Use a card to represent letter combinations (consonant blends) such as *fr*—to reinforce words such as *frog, from, free*.

- Use this game as an icebreaker to teach children the art of non-verbal communication. Have the children play the game in silence, using body language, facial expressions, and gestures to show what letter combinations they want to make.

- Have teams keep their own scores. When one team presents its tally, the other teams verify the totals. This integrates mathematics into the play and learning of a vocabulary game. In grades 1 to 3, addition is a new skill, and this format reinforces the skill through play and practice.

- Consider using a noisemaker, such as a call bell, to indicate the end of a round or to announce that a team has created a special word.

- Conduct as a floor game. Have the letter carriers stand and hold the card and then create formations that spell out words, similar to fans at a sports event spelling out a cheer.

CUSTOMIZING ALPHABET SOUP

Size of Group
- For one player:

  Time Driven

  - Establish a standard time.

  - Challenge student to match or better the stated time.

  - Tally how many times the student is able to match or better the standard.

  Quantity Driven

  - Establish a standard score.

  - Challenge student to match or better the score within a stated or an open time period.

- For medium and large groups:

  - For groups of ten to twenty students: Form two or three teams of six to eight players each. This will encourage healthy competition yet allow you to control the play.

  - For larger groups of older students: Hand out more than one set of letter series; use several sets of *a, b, e, s, t* and *a, b, d, e, r* and *a, e, m, r, s*. Have the teams play simultaneously, with the recorders writing down each word. Collect the word lists at the end of the round.

Time of Play
- Shorten or lengthen the time allowed in relation to the difficulty of the letter set.

Focus of the Task
- Include one or two additional letter cards.

- Give two cards to each player. This allows more flexibility of play yet maintains small group size.

- Create a wildcard that teams can use as any letter in the alphabet. Have the recorder write down the entire word, including the letter represented by the wild card.

- Post pictures or give out clues to possible word combinations.

Scoring

- Award 30 bonus points if a team creates a preselected "bonus" word or words. This word might be seasonal (a holiday item) or curricular. For instance, inform the players that there are one or more "secret" word combinations related to the lesson that will receive bonus points. If the letters the team has are *a, b, d, e, r* and if your lesson stresses homophonic, or sound-alike, words, you could use *bare* and *bear* as your bonus words. (Use a noisemaker to announce that a team has found a bonus word.)

- Award a bonus of 1 point for each word formed.

- Award bonus points for neatness of the word lists submitted by recorders.

- As necessary, give partial credit for misspelled words, such as *ba* for *baa* (sound made by sheep), and so forth.

Alphabet Soup

a, b, e, s, t (32 words)

five-letter words:	abets, baste, bates, beast, beats
four-letter words:	abet, base, bast, bate, bats, beat, best, bets, east, eats, sate, seat, stab, tabs, teas
three-letter words:	ate, bat, bet, eat, sat, sea, set, tab, tea
two-letter words:	as, at, be

a, b, d, e, r (28 words)

five-letter words:	bared, beard, bread, debar
four-letter words:	abed, bade, bard, bare, bead, bear, brad, brae, bred, dare, dear, drab, read
three-letter words:	are, bad, bar, bed, bra, dab, ear, era, red
two-letter words:	ad, be

a, f, l, o, t (18 words)

five-letter words:	aloft, float
four-letter words:	alto, flat, foal, loaf, loft
three-letter words:	ace, aft, cad, den, fat, lot, oaf, oat, oft
two-letter words:	ad, an

a, c, h, r, s (17 words)

five-letter words:	chars, crash
four-letter words:	arch, arcs, cars, cash, char, rash, scar
three-letter words:	arc, ash, car, has, sac
two-letter words:	ah, as, ha

a, e, f, s, t (23 words)

five-letter words:	fates, feast, feats
four-letter words:	east, eats, fast, fate, fats, feat, safe, sate, seat, teas
three-letter words:	aft, ate, eat, fat, sat, set, tea
two-letter words:	as, at, fa

a, e, l, p, s (32 words)

five-letter words:	lapse, leaps, pales, peals, pleas
four-letter words:	ales, alps, apes, laps, leap, pale, pals, peal, peas, pleas, sale, seal, slap
three-letter words:	ale, alp, ape, asp, lap, lea, pal, pea, sap, sea, spa
two-letter words:	as, la, pa

a, e, m, r, s (27 words)

five-letter words:	mares, maser, reams, smear
four-letter words:	arms, ears, eras, mare, mars, mesa, rams, ream, same, seam, sear,
three-letter words:	are, arm, ear, era, mare, ram, sea
two-letter words:	am, as, ma, me, re

a, e, f, m, r (17 words)

five-letter words:	frame
four-letter words:	fame, fare, farm, fear, mare, ream
three-letter words:	are, arm, ear, ear, far, mar, ram, ref
two-letter words:	am, re

Alphabet Soup

a, e, g, m, s (17 words)

five-letter words:	games
four-letter words:	ages, game, gems, mesa, sage, same, seam
three-letter words:	age, gas, gem, sag, sea
two-letter words:	am, as, ma, me

a, e, g, r, t (24 words)

five-letter words:	grate, great
four-letter words:	gate, gear, rage, rate, tare, tear
three-letter words:	age, are, art, ate, ear, eat, era, gar, get, rag, rat, tag, tar, tea
two-letter words:	at, re

a, e, i, l, s (20 words)

five-letter words:	aisle
four-letter words:	ails, ales, isle, ilea, leas, leis, lies, sail, sale, seal
three-letter words:	ail, ale, lea, lei, lie, sea
two-letter words:	as, is, la

a, e, l, n, r (17 words)

five-letter words:	learn, renal
four-letter words:	earl, earn, lane, lean, near, real
three-letter words:	ale, are, ear, era, lea, ran
two-letter words:	an, la, re

a, e, r, t, t (18 words)

five-letter words:	tetra, treat
four-letter words:	rate, tare, tart, tear, teat
three-letter words:	are, art, ate, ear, eat, era, rat, tar, tat, tea
two-letter words:	at

e, i, r, s, t (23 words)

five-letter words:	rites, tiers, tires, tries
four-letter words:	erst, ires, rest, rise, rite, sire, site, stir, tier, ties, tire
three-letter words:	ire, its, set, sir, sit, tie
two-letter words:	is, it

e, h, o, r, s (18 words)

five-letter words:	horse, shore
four-letter words:	hero, hers, hoes, hose, ores, roes, rose, shoe, sore
three-letter words:	her, hoe, ore, roe, she
two-letter words:	or, so

h, o, r, t, w (16 words)

five-letter words:	throw, worth, wroth
four-letter words:	wort
three-letter words:	hot, how, rot, row, tow, two, who
two-letter words:	at, ah, ho, oh, or

Alphabet Soup

5-letter words = 25 points
4-letter words = 15 points
3-letter words = 7 points
2-letter words = 3 points

Round	Team	Team	Team
1	___ × 25 = ___ × 15 = ___ × 7 = ___ × 3 =	___ × 25 = ___ × 15 = ___ × 7 = ___ × 3 =	___ × 25 = ___ × 15 = ___ × 7 = ___ × 3 =
2	___ × 25 = ___ × 15 = ___ × 7 = ___ × 3 =	___ × 25 = ___ × 15 = ___ × 7 = ___ × 3 =	___ × 25 = ___ × 15 = ___ × 7 = ___ × 3 =
3	___ × 25 = ___ × 15 = ___ × 7 = ___ × 3 =	___ × 25 = ___ × 15 = ___ × 7 = ___ × 3 =	___ × 25 = ___ × 15 = ___ × 7 = ___ × 3 =
4	___ × 25 = ___ × 15 = ___ × 7 = ___ × 3 =	___ × 25 = ___ × 15 = ___ × 7 = ___ × 3 =	___ × 25 = ___ × 15 = ___ × 7 = ___ × 3 =
Total Points			

Alphabet Soup

- Form into teams of six or more players.

- Select a *recorder* and five *letter carriers.*

- Give each letter carrier one letter card.

- When told to start, your letter carriers have three minutes to form as many words as they can with the assigned letter cards.

- Words earn these scores:

    2-letter words = 3 points

    3-letter words = 7 points

    4-letter words = 15 points

    5-letter words = 25 points

- The team with the most points wins.

AT RISK

INTRODUCTION At Risk offers a secure environment in which children can both have fun reviewing their topic knowledge and learn some life lessons about risk and consequence. After the teacher asks a question, the first player in each group who thinks he knows the answer covers his head with his hand, and everyone else quickly copies him. The last player to cover is *at risk*. This activity keeps everyone involved and participating at some level. The right answer earns the first player a chip and costs the at risk player a chip. Useful opportunities to discuss issues of fairness, honesty, and cooperation can also arise when children play At Risk.

| **Purpose** | • To foster understanding of the topic. |
| | • To introduce the rewards and consequences of risk taking. |

| **Game Objective** | To have the most chips or tokens at the end of the game. |

| **Players** | 3 or more. *Can be adapted for one-on-one tutoring.* |

| **Time** | 10–30 minutes. |

| **Grades** | 3–8. |

Supplies	• Set of questions, prepared in advance by the teacher.
	• 4 chips per player plus 1 chip for each group.
	• 1 paper cup per group

GAME STEPS

Preliminaries	• Divide class into groups of five to seven players.
	• Have each group sit on the floor in a circle or at its own table.
	• Place one paper cup containing one chip in center of each floor circle or table.
	• Distribute four chips to each player.

Game Play: Round 1

Read the first question aloud or display it on the overhead.

- The first player in each group who thinks she knows the correct response places her hand on the top of her head.

- Once the first player covers her head, every other player must cover her head.

- The last player to cover her head is at risk.

- Ask the first player who covered her head in each group to respond to the question.

Scoring

For a *correct response*, the first player takes 1 chip from the paper cup *and* the at risk player puts 1 chip in the paper cup

For an *incorrect response*, the first player puts 1 chip in the paper cup

Round 2 to End of Game

Play continues in this fashion until the end of the game.

End of Game

The player with the most chips in each group is declared the winner of that group.

SCORING EXAMPLE

Preliminaries

- The class is divided into groups of five to seven players.

- Each group is seated at a table.

- A paper cup with one chip is placed in the middle of the table.

- Each player receives four chips.

Round 1: Table 1

- The teacher presents the first question.
- Player 3 is the first player at Table 1 to indicate that he knows the answer by covering his head—he places his hand on top of his head.
- All players at Table 1 race to cover their heads.
- Player 5 is the last player to cover his head. Player 5 is at risk.
- The teacher instructs all first players to state their response.
- Player 3 states his response to his group.
- The teacher presents the correct response.
- Player 3's response is correct.
- Player 3 takes one chip from the paper cup.
- Player 5 puts one of his chips into the paper cup.
- This ends play for Round 1.

Round 2: Table 1

- The teacher presents the second question.
- Player 2 is the first player to cover her head.
- Player 4 is the last player to cover her head. Player 4 is at risk.
- The teacher instructs all first players to state their response.
- Player 2 gives her response to the question.
- The teacher presents the correct response.
- Player 2's response is incorrect.
- Player 2 puts one of her chips into the paper cup.
- This ends play for Round 2.

TEACHER NOTES

- It is never too early to learn about taking risks. Use this game to offer players a chance to risk, and fail, in a playful environment.

- Try this game as a means of accelerating interest in material that is important but tedious to memorize, such as state capitals, multiplication tables, and the alphabet. The added fun of being the first one to touch one's head engages the student with the content.

- Use this game to deal with issues of fairness, honesty, and cooperation. Children who are last may claim to have covered their head before other players. Younger students may have a hard time with the fairness issue. You may hear complaints such as: "Tommy touched his head last!" "No, Samantha did!" If this is a problem, try to bring in adult volunteers or a teacher's aid to monitor the game. You might even want to pick student monitors. Make a big deal out of it. Let them wear a special hat and "induct" them. Rotate the assignment so that all the students who want to be a monitor get the chance.

- Play on the floor. This is the perfect game to be played on the floor, especially for younger students. Simply have the students sit in a circle and place the paper cup in the middle. Getting students out of their seats and in a new situation gets their brains moving, too. Brain research studies have shown that the brain works better when the body is able to move every twenty minutes or so. By getting students physically out of their chairs, and on the floor, you allow for this movement. Finally, personal interaction is encouraged when a table does not obstruct players.

- This game keeps all players on their toes—not just the first player to respond to the question. This encourages children to become actively involved in learning and not be just spectators.

- Some children may need a round or two to get used to the dynamics of the game. But once they do, you will find that this will become a favorite review activity.

- Completing two tasks at the same time—thinking about the answer and covering their heads—may be difficult for children in the K–2 grades, but it is a wonderful way to challenge their skills and stretch their thinking. If your students are having coordination difficulties use easier questions for the first few rounds. This will give children a chance to practice the motor aspect of the game. Then, as they become more comfortable with the physical tasks, increase the difficulty level of the questions.

- If you use a true-false variation (in which all students respond by covering their heads when they think a response is "true"), observe how children are swayed by the overt responses of their classmates. You may want to discuss the issue of influence during the closing of the game.

- Children who may not wish to volunteer information can still be actively involved in the playing of this game and become winners. This emphasizes that paying attention to the activity within your group is as important as knowing the correct answer.

- Discuss the difference between knowing the information and active participation in the game (covering your head).

- For older, larger groups: Have the first player write down his response and then compare this response to the correct answer.

- Use this game as a small-group activity for students who are finished early with their work. Touching the head is, or should be, a silent activity. Set up a table on the outskirts of the classroom so children can play this game while others are working.

- For younger children: Use this game as a means of identifying different body parts. Have children touch their elbows or their knees instead of covering their heads.

- For elementary language classrooms: Use this game to test and reinforce foreign language phrases dealing with different parts of the body. The French teacher might announce, "touchez votre nez" ("touch your nose"), for example, to determine how well the students understand the basics of the language.

- For smaller groups: Use a noisemaker (ring a bell, for example) when one of the players has covered his or her head. This will add to the excitement of the game.

- If you cannot locate poker-type chips, use any type of token, such as paper clips, precut pieces of paper, pennies, ticket stubs, or bingo markers.

- The most economical and disposable cup is usually the four-ounce bathroom cup. But, you may use Styrofoam cups, mugs, or any available small receptacle. If nothing is available, mark off an area in the middle of the players' circle and designate it as the area where the chips go.

CUSTOMIZING AT RISK

Size of Group

- For one or two players:

    - Present a question and then give a response. If the player believes the response is correct, he covers his head. If the player believes the response is incorrect, he remains still.

    - See if the player(s) can "survive" eleven rounds of play, then extend the goal to fifteen rounds, or more.

- For one group of players: Present a question and proceed as described in the game steps.

- For larger groups: Divide students into several groups of five to seven players as described earlier. Make sure that each group is keeping up with the play of the game—covering their heads, hearing the correct response, and being awarded or turning in chips.

Time of Play

- Shorten or lengthen the game in accordance with the topic and available time.

Focus of the Task

- Vary the questions by using different question formats, mixing topics, or inserting questions on information not fully covered in class.

- Present a true-false round, in which players cover their heads if they agree with the response and keep their hands at their sides if they do not agree. Chips are awarded or turned in in accordance with the quality of the response.

- Introduce an unordered set of objects. The first player to see how to place them in correct order covers her head.

- Once any player has turned in all of her chips, she is eliminated from play.

- Play the game until only one player has one or no chips left.

- Place a paper cup mouth-down at the center of the circle or the table. The first player covers the cup instead of his head.

- For a single group: Place a call bell at the center of the circle or table. The first player who rings the bell puts all other players at risk.

Scoring

- To encourage more competition, award two chips for correct responses. To discourage competition, reward 0 chips.

- Use challenge play. Allow any player who was not the first player to challenge the response given at his table. Award one chip to the challenging player if he is correct.

- Distribute only three chips to each player. When those chips are gone, the player must leave the game.

- Have each group compete as a team. Have one player represent each team, in the center of the room. Conduct the game as usual, but conduct the scoring on a team basis. Or try this variation: announce the topic of the question and allow each team to select its "expert" representative. Require that each team rotate its representatives.

At Risk

- Divide into groups of five to seven players.

- Each player receives four chips.

- Teacher presents a question.

- The first player who thinks he or she knows the correct response covers his or her head with one hand.

- All other players in the group quickly cover their heads.

- The last player to cover is *at risk.*

- The first player responds to the question.

- Responses earn these scores:

  For a *correct response,* the first player takes 1 chip from the paper cup *and* the at risk player puts 1 chip in the paper cup.

  For an *incorrect response,* the first player puts 1 chip in the paper cup.

- Play is the same for each question. At the end the player with the most chips wins.

BALLOON JUGGLE

INTRODUCTION   Balloon Juggle is a great game for special days, when students' energy levels are high. Players must keep a balloon in the air while they respond to a question. Points are awarded to teams both on the quality of the response and for keeping the balloon aloft. This game also gives the students who are good at athletics a chance to stand out in the classroom. It works on both motor and mental skills, gives students a constructive reason to be active, and can easily be made more demanding for older students.

Purpose	• To reinforce players' understanding and ability to apply information in a stressful situation.
	• To increase both mental and physical agility.

Game Objective	To score the most points.

Players	2 or more. *Can be adapted for one-on-one tutoring.*

Time	10–30 minutes.

Grades	2–8.

Supplies	• A set of questions, prepared in advance by the teacher.
	• 3 or more inflated balloons.

GAME STEPS

Preliminaries	• Divide class into two or three teams.
	• Have first team send up one player.

Round 1	• Hand an inflated balloon to the player.
	• Present the first question.
	• The player tries to keep the balloon in the air while responding to the question.

Scoring

Responding *correctly* and keeping the balloon in the air = 7 points

Responding *correctly* but dropping the balloon = 3 points

Responding *incorrectly* but keeping the balloon in the air = 3 points

Responding *incorrectly* and dropping the balloon = 0 points

- Record the first team's score on the chalkboard.

Round 2 to End of Game

- All rounds are played in the same manner.

End of Game

- The team with the most points is declared the winner.

SCORING EXAMPLE

Preliminaries

- The class is divided into two teams.
- Team A goes first.

Round 1: Team A

- The first player from Team A receives a balloon. The player puts the balloon in the air. The teacher presents the first math problem: 2 + 13 − 1 = ?
- While keeping the balloon in the air, the player responds, "14." The response is *correct,* and the player *kept the balloon aloft.*
- The teacher awards 7 points to Team A.

	Team A
Round 1	7

Round 1: Team B

- The first player from Team B receives a balloon. The player puts the balloon in the air. The teacher presents the second math problem: $24 + 6 - 1 = ?$

- The player drops the balloon and responds, "29." The response is *correct,* but the player *dropped the balloon.*

- The teacher awards 3 points to Team B.

	Team A	Team B
Round 1	7	3

Round 2: Team A

- The second player from Team A puts the balloon in the air. The teacher presents the third math problem: $21 - 2 + 9 = ?$

- The player drops the balloon and responds, "26." The response is *incorrect,* and the player *dropped the balloon.*

- The teacher awards 0 points to Team A.

	Team A	Team B
Round 1	7	3
Round 2	0	

Round 2: Team B

- The second player from Team B puts the balloon in the air. The teacher presents the fourth math problem: $17 + 4 - 6 = ?$

- The player drops the balloon and responds, "15." The response is *correct,* but the player *dropped the balloon.*

- The teacher awards 3 points to Team B.

	Team A	Team B
Round 1	7	3
Round 2	0	3
Total Points	7	6

TEACHER NOTES

- When using balloons be *very careful* that children do not poke or bite into a balloon. A popped balloon can become a hazard, especially if near the mouth and nose. One precautionary step is to slightly underinflate the balloons.

- As this game involves using motor skills while retrieving facts, two parts of the brain are working at the same time. This helps children open up new parts of their minds and may possibly open up new skills and a new way of looking at things.

- Some children who are lagging behind in their studies may be very skilled athletically. This game will give them a chance to shine and to feel good about their skills. You can build on this good feeling and encourage these students to take on new intellectual challenges. They will soon learn that keeping the balloon aloft is only half the battle. If they know the correct response *and* are able to keep the balloons up, they will have an advantage over the students who have the book knowledge but are having a hard time with the juggling.

- Use this game as an intellectual diversion from decorating for a party. Take a break from decorating and use one of the balloon decorations for your game and then return to decorating or enjoy the festivities.

- Use a noisemaker to signal the end of a round of play or a special occurrence such as correctly responding to an especially difficult question.

- Some teachers may think that bouncing a balloon equals chaos. If you find that students are becoming disruptive with their balloons, you may add the game rule that disruptive behavior or misuse of the balloon will result in losing a turn. This will emphasize that play within the rules is the only way to win.

- Consider adding an additional balloon to the juggling task for older children. Ask for volunteer jugglers before you proceed. This will help you determine if the additional balloon is a fair challenge for this grade level.

- This is a fun game for *special days*—those days before a long vacation or a day with a school assembly or class party. This game also may be used on those days when students seem to have a hard time sitting down and doing their regular work.

- Use this game when working with children who have extra energy or children who simply need to move and fidget while thinking. Players, and observers, will be so focused on the question and the juggle that they will have little time to get into a disruptive pattern.

- This game reinforces the concept that energy is a good thing and that classrooms are good places to expend that energy.

- Allow teams to practice their juggling by placing the players in a circle and having them bounce the balloon player-to-player around the circle. This builds team spirit and increases players' familiarity with the task.

- Assign teams a balloon of a specific color. This reinforces team identity and, for younger children, knowledge of colors as the teams are identified as the Red Team, Blue Team, and the like.

- To increase the skill level, require teams of older students to juggle their balloons as they walk an obstacle course of three or four chairs while responding to a series of questions.

CUSTOMIZING BALLOON JUGGLE

Size of Group

- For one player:

    - Have the player keep one balloon in the air while responding to a series of questions. The round stops after one minute or if the player drops the balloon.

    - Have the player keep the balloon in the air while walking around a chair as you ask one or more questions.

- For larger groups:

    - Have one team play at a time while other teams observe.

    - Using handpicked observers or assistants, have several teams play head-to-head simultaneously.

| **Time of Play** | • Shorten or lengthen the time period as appropriate to the difficulty of the questions or number of players. |

| **Focus of the Task** | • To introduce or reinforce team play, give a team two balloons and require team members to keep the balloons aloft as they respond to questions. This will reinforce the concept of cooperation as well as cover the material. |

• To reinforce general motor skills, have players walk an obstacle course while keeping a balloon aloft.

• To give students practice in public speaking, have them introduce themselves or read from a statement while keeping a balloon in the air.

• Have teams run a balloon race. The first-place team receives 3 points for a correct answer; the second-place team receives 2 points, and so on.

• To reinforce coordination skills, have players do a simple task, such as solving a math problem on the chalkboard while keeping one balloon aloft.

• Have a player answer a series of questions until she misses the first question or drops the balloon, or have all the players on a team answer questions until they answer incorrectly or drop the one or two balloons they are passing around in a circle.

| **Scoring** | • For older students or during *play-off* rounds: Award points only for correct responses *and* for keeping the balloon aloft. This underscores the importance of multitasking. |

• Ask questions that each require several responses. Give 1 point for each correct response. The round ends when time expires or the player drops a balloon or gives an incorrect response.

• Award a bonus if a team responds correctly to all questions.

Balloon Juggle

Correct while balloon is in air = 7 points
Incorrect while balloon is in air = 3 points
Correct but balloon is dropped = 3 points
Incorrect and balloon is dropped = 0 points

Round	Team	Team	Team
1			
2			
3			
4			
5			
Total Points			

Balloon Juggle

- Divide into two or three teams.

- The first player puts the balloon in the air.

- The player is asked a question.

- The player responds while trying to keep the balloon in the air.

- Scoring is as follows:

  Responding *correctly* and keeping the balloon in the air = 7 points

  Responding *correctly* but dropping the balloon = 3 points

  Responding *incorrectly* but keeping the balloon in the air = 3 points

  Responding *incorrectly* and dropping the balloon = 0 points

- Play is the same for all rounds, and the team with the most points wins.

BATTER UP!

INTRODUCTION

Batter Up!, a baseball-style game played by two teams, offers many opportunities for involving students in academic material and also encourages concepts of teamwork. A team sends up a *batter* to respond to a question. A correct answer is a *hit*, and an incorrect one is an *out.* A team's players stay at bat answering questions and moving around the bases on a game sheet until the team receives three outs. Students can also easily participate in this game as monitors and scorers, working on practical math skills and learning about responsibility.

| **Purpose** | • To strengthen understanding of a topic by answering questions in a competitive game format. |
| | • To practice real-life math skills. |

| **Game Objective** | To score the most runs. |

| **Players** | 4 or more. *Can be adapted for one-on-one tutoring.* |

| **Time** | 15–45 minutes. |

| **Grades** | 3–8. |

Supplies	• A set of questions, prepared in advance by the teacher.
	• A wall chart of the baseball playing field and scoreboard (shown as a game sheet at the end of this game).
	• 1 Batter Up! score sheet.
	• 1 set of markers—made of colored paper, for example, to represent base runners—for each team.
	• Index cards marked "1 out," "2 outs," and "3 outs" to indicate number of outs.
	• Masking tape, to attach markers to scoreboard.

GAME STEPS

| **Preliminaries** | • Divide class into two teams. |
| | • Have each team line up in single file. |

Inning 1: Team A Is At Bat.

- Ask the first question of the first player for Team A.

- First player responds to the question.

A *correct* response = a *hit* and the player is awarded first base

An *incorrect* response = an *out*

- This completes first player's turn. The next player is now at bat.

Scoring

4 *hits* by 1 team in an inning = 1 *run*.

Each additional *hit* by the team in the inning = 1 *run*.

- Continue play in this fashion until Team A has three outs.

- Tally the runs scored by Team A on the score sheet.

Inning 1: Team B Is At Bat.

- Play is the same as in the first half of the inning.

Inning 2 to End of Game

- Each inning is played in the same fashion.

End of Game

- The team with the most runs is declared the winner.

SCORING EXAMPLE

Preliminaries

- The class is divided into two teams: Team A and Team B.

- Team A is first to go to bat.

Inning 1: Team A Is At Bat.

- The teacher presents the first question. The first player's response is correct. The player gets a hit. The teacher awards the player first base by placing the team's marker on the base on the game sheet. This completes the first player's turn.

- The teacher presents the second question. The second player's response is incorrect. The second player gets an out. The teacher places the "1 out" card in the appropriate area of the wall chart. This completes the second player's turn.

- The teacher presents the third question. The third player's response is correct. The player gets a hit. The teacher awards a base by placing the team's marker on second base. This completes the third player's turn.

- The teacher presents the fourth question. The fourth player's response is correct. The player gets a hit. The teacher awards a base by placing the team's marker on third base. This completes the fourth player's turn.

- The teacher presents the fifth question. The fifth player's response is incorrect. The player gets an out. The teacher places the "2 outs" card in the appropriate area of the flipchart. This completes the fifth player's turn.

- The teacher presents the sixth question. The sixth player's response is correct. The player gets a hit. The teacher awards the team its fourth hit by marking one run under Team A's score. This completes the sixth player's turn.

- The teacher presents the seventh question. The seventh player's response is incorrect. The player gets an out. The teacher places the "3 outs" card in the appropriate area of the wall chart. This completes the seventh player's turn.

- This completes Team A's first inning.

- The teacher marks "1 run" in the appropriate section of the wall chart.

Inning 1: Team B Is At Bat.

- This portion of inning 1 is played in the same fashion.

- The teacher marks Team B's runs on the wall chart.

End of Inning 1
- The teacher notes both teams' scores.

TEACHER NOTES

- This game gets children out of their seats while still focusing on learning.

- The technique of not scoring until the fourth hit of the inning mirrors real baseball play (most of the hits in baseball are singles, or one-base hits) and encourages team play because each student can be only partially responsible for the total effort and success of the team.

- This is a good game for younger grades, even when reading skills are not yet developed. As the teacher presents the question, he can reinforce the student in the meaning of the question and the appropriateness of the correct response.

- When you need a large number of questions for a game like this one, one tip is to write a few questions each day on the learning unit. This will keep the facts and objectives fresh in your mind throughout the unit. By writing down questions from the beginning of your studies, you will cover all of your lessons.

- Create a mix of questions of varying difficulty if you have children of different ages competing in the same game.

- Create a series of questions that are increasingly difficult. Use the easier questions in the first inning, and increase the complexity of the questions in each subsequent inning.

- When a player is having trouble with the questions, inform him that the league's best pitcher is on the mound.

- When you want to introduce more difficult questions after a couple of innings, inform each team that the opposing team is bringing in its *relief pitcher.*

- Assign one or more students to be *official scorers* and to keep track of the hits, outs, and runs. Your validation of their totals will reinforce their numerical skills.

- Assign one or more students to be *pitchers* or question readers. These students can come from the playing teams or from an observers group (the *bleachers*).

- Encourage older students to keep their own batting average (number of hits divided by total times at bat). This emphasizes the use of math and statistics in everyday life.

- Consider pairing each player with a fellow team member to respond to a question. This pairing can be random or designed to create partnerships between students of differing intellectual abilities. The student needing extra help benefits from the student who easily understands the concepts, and the student who understands the concepts benefits from demonstrating knowledge and coaching skills.

- Play *preseason* games to allow students to learn the rules of the game in a more relaxed environment.

- Use a noisemaker, such as a call bell, when a player gets a hit or to announce the end of an inning of play.

- Establish a more complete baseball environment by doing any or all of the following:

  - Introduce this game at the beginning of the spring baseball season or in the fall to mirror the play-off and World Series games.

  - Create a *batter's box* by having each player stand at a *home plate* while responding to questions. Allow the player in the batter's box to hold a plastic bat.

  - Create an infield by placing four bases around the room. Players can move around the bases and score runs, as directed.

- Take the game outside to the playground or into the school gym. Have each player getting a hit move to first base and then around the bases to score on a teammate's hit.

- Allow teams to wear baseball hats and tags indicating their selected team name.

- Have one player from the opposing team act as pitcher and read the question aloud to the batter.

- Have teams sing "Take Me Out to the Ballgame" before playing the first inning or when a portion of an inning is completed.

- Create an ongoing *league* with four or more teams and keep a win-lose record for the *season*. Any nonplaying teams can become spectators in the bleachers. Establish a play-off schedule.

- Have a member of the class write up the game for the *sports section* of your class or school newspaper.

- Have snacks of peanuts and Cracker Jack on the day of the big game.

- Invite other classes to watch a play-off game if appropriate.

CUSTOMIZING BATTER UP!

Size of Group
- For one player: Establish a standard number of hits and of runs per inning and then have the student compete against that standard. Make a diagram of a baseball field or photocopy the game sheet provided and then play at the student's desk or table. Use markers, such as pieces of colored paper, self-stick paper notes, or paper tags to indicate the student's movement around the bases. Allow the player three outs so he can score more hits and runs.

- For one player or small groups:

  - Use a photocopy of the game sheet as the game board.

- For larger groups:

  - Select two teams and have *bleacher seats* for additional students. These students can also serve as scorekeepers and pitchers to read questions to the batters.

  - Create three teams and revise the batting format to allow all three teams to bat per inning.

Time of Play

- Shorten period of play by keeping game to one inning. Expand period of play by adding more innings, as required.

- Shorten or lengthen time allowed for the response to a question.

- Play one inning a day for a week. Keep the interim scores posted, and announce the weeklong winners on the final day.

Focus of the Task

- Create a more active game by marking a batter's box on the floor (perhaps with masking tape). Have the player at bat stand in the batter's box to respond to the question. If the player makes a hit, have him place his team's marker on first base and advance the other markers, as required.

- Pair players with a fellow team member to respond to a question, as described earlier.

- Have one player from the opposing team act as pitcher and read the question to the batting player.

- Have each batter read the question and then respond. This will offer players' practice in reading comprehension as well as deepening understanding of the material.

- Have older students prepare questions on index cards about the lesson material. Mix these questions with your questions, and use the mix for the game.

- Create sets of question cards in different categories or formats. Indicate the category or format in each pile, and each time a new team comes to bat, allow the opposing team to select the question set that will be used.

Scoring

- Assign variable scores to the questions—moderate questions earn one base, multiple or more difficult questions earn extra bases.

- Have the batter select the value of a question (one base or extra bases) prior to the presentation of the question.

- For quicker scoring, count all correct answers as two-base hits and award the inning's first run on the second hit.

Batter Up!

Inning	Away Team	Home Team
1	Hits _____ Runs _____	Hits _____ Runs _____
2	Hits _____ Runs _____	Hits _____ Runs _____
3	Hits _____ Runs _____	Hits _____ Runs _____
4	Hits _____ Runs _____	Hits _____ Runs _____
5	Hits _____ Runs _____	Hits _____ Runs _____
Total Scores	Hits _____ Runs _____	Hits _____ Runs _____

Batter Up!

Inning	1	2	3	4	5
Team:					
Team:					

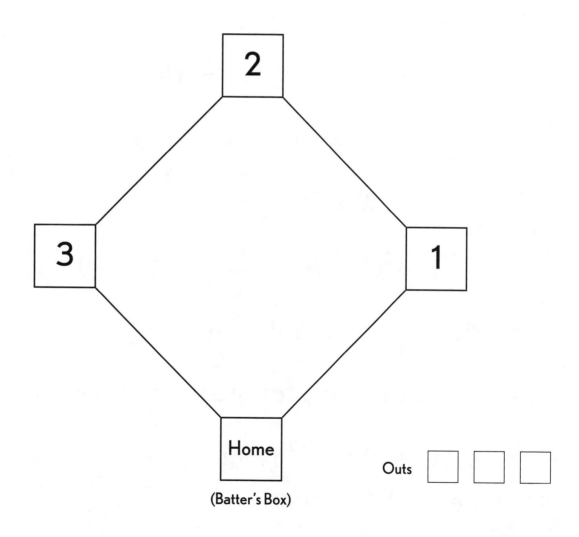

(Batter's Box)

Batter Up!

- Divide into two teams.

- The first batter on the first team responds to the first question.

- Scoring is as follows:

    A *correct* response = a *hit*

    An *incorrect* response = an *out*

    The first 4 hits = 1 *run*

    Each hit after the first 4 = 1 *run*

- Play continues until Team A gets three outs.

- Play is the same for the second team.

- At the end of all the innings, the team with the most runs wins.

Bingo 1: Letter Bingo

INTRODUCTION

Letter Bingo encourages students to engage in critical thinking and problem solving as they actively build their vocabularies. Each team receives a Bingo-style game sheet with one letter or letter group in each square. The teacher presents a clue to a word, and the team must first solve the clue and then mark the letter that players think begins that word. The goal is to be the first to cover four squares in a vertical, horizontal, or corner-to-corner diagonal row. The game can also be played with numbers and is adaptable to many topics and all primary grades.

This game, the score cards and blank cards, and the variations presented are adapted from *Framegames by Thiagi,* 7th Edition, by S. Thiagarajan. See other games and ideas by Thiagarajan on his Web site, www.thiagi@thiagi.com.

| **Purpose** | • To strengthen the association between letters and topic items. |
| | • To reinforce vocabulary and spelling skills. |

| **Game Objective** | To win by covering 4 game board squares in a horizontal, vertical, or diagonal (corner-to-corner) row. |

| **Players** | 4 or more. *Can be adapted for one-on-one tutoring.* |

| **Time** | 15–45 minutes. |

| **Grades** | K–8. |

Supplies	• A set of questions and clues about the topic.
	• 1 game sheet per team.
	• 1 marker (coin or chip or other small token) per team.
	• Paper and pencils for each team.

GAME STEPS

| **Preliminaries** | • Divide class into teams of two or three players each. |
| | • Distribute one game sheet and one marker to each team. |

Round 1	• Present a word or picture clue.
	• Have teams place their markers on the game sheet letter representing the correct response.
	• Announce the correct response.

Scoring

For a *correct* response, the team removes its marker *and* marks an "X" through the correct square.

For an *incorrect* response, the team removes its marker.

This completes the first round of play.

Round 2 to End of Game

Play is the same for each round.

End of Game

The first team to cover four squares in a row is declared the winner.

SCORING EXAMPLE

Preliminaries

- The class is divided into teams of two to three players.

- Each team receives a marker and a game sheet:

B	O	K	H
E	D	J	P
M	J	F	C
G	N	L	A

- Students are instructed to find the first letter of the words represented by the clues given by the teacher.

Round 1

- The teacher reads the first clue: "What is the first letter of the long-legged, swiftest of all the wild cats who live in Africa?"

- Team A thinks "cheetah," and places its marker on the "C" square:

B	O	K	H
E	D	J	P
M	J	F	Ⓒ
G	N	L	A

- The teacher calls time and gives the correct response: "cheetah."

- All players remove their markers from the game sheet.

- Those teams who correctly select "C" cross off that square.

- Team A crosses off the "C":

B	O	K	H
E	D	J	P
M	J	F	✗
G	N	L	A

Round 2

- The teacher reads the second clue: "What is the first letter of the city that is the capital of Texas?"

- Team A thinks "Dallas" and places its marker on the "D":

B	O	K	H
E	Ⓓ	J	P
M	J	F	✗
G	N	L	A

- The teacher calls time and gives the correct response: "Austin."

- All teams, including Team A, remove their markers from the game sheet.

- The teams who correctly selected "A" cross out that square.

- Because Team A's response was incorrect, its game sheet remains unchanged after Round 2:

B	O	K	H
E	D	J	P
M	J	F	⨯
G	N	L	A

TEACHER NOTES

- Use this game to bring energy and fun to reinforcing vocabulary and spelling skills. Instead of engaging in mindless memorization, students are demonstrating their understanding by associating an initial letter with an item. When you present a picture of a bird and then ask teams to cover the appropriate letter, the students demonstrate their understanding by covering the letter. Reinforcement happens when you review and elaborate on the correct response with the class.

- Supplement a homework assignment with this game. By providing responses to a list of clues, students demonstrate critical thinking and problem solving.

- Consider this game as another way to involve children who may be having a hard time with the concept of letter and word association. Because of its level of player involvement and reliance on varied methods of communications (visual, oral, kinesthetic) the game appeals to learners with varied learning styles.

- For foreign language students: Say a word in the foreign language or demonstrate the word by pantomiming or by holding up a picture, and then have the students cover the appropriate word on the sheet.

- For younger students: Create game sheets with one word in each square. Present a picture or a verbal description or definition and then have the students cover the appropriate square.

- For younger students: Use this game to

  - K: Introduce letters at end of the year.

  - 1: Introduce capital and lowercase letters at the end of the year.

  - 2–3: Increase familiarity with script letters.

- For older students: Use this game to problem solve with clues associated with one letter:

  - Chemistry: ask for symbol of nitrogen (N).

  - Spelling: ask for the silent letter in "know."

  - General knowledge: ask for the word (or just the letter) associated with a popular hot beverage made from leaves (tea, or "T").

- The recommended team size is from two to three. You will find that teams larger than three have problems coordinating the decision making and square selection in the time required.

- If several teams win simultaneously, consider using a variety of game sheets that present the same letters in differing arrangements, to stagger the scoring.

- Create your own variations on copies of the blank game sheets found at the end of this game.

- If a team gets Bingo before you have completed your lesson, stop the game and congratulate the players, and then continue play.

- Have extra game sheets in case children make an error by crossing out the wrong game square.

- Use this game when you want to group players in teams to encourage them to share and to compare their responses for non-threatening reinforcement.

- When teams are involved in a *self-scoring* game, cheating or the appearance of cheating may become an issue. If a team's players are accused by other teams of giving themselves a square they did not earn, the teacher should deflect the focus from the team involved and invoke a discussion of fair play. Discussion of questions such as, "would you do *anything* to win?" or, "what if you saw someone cheating or stealing?" might become one of most important learning moments of the game.

CUSTOMIZING LETTER BINGO

Size of Group

- For one player: Establish a standard time. Challenge the student to cover as many squares as possible on the game sheet within that time.

- For larger groups: Consider placing clues on the chalkboard or on an overhead projector.

Time of Play

- Shorten or lengthen the time of each round in relation to the difficulty of the association between the clue and the letter.

- Shorten the game to getting three squares in a row.

Focus of the Task

- Create variations of the four-by-four grid. The most popular is the Tic-Tac-Toe, or three-by-three, grid, because it plays quickly and is easier to complete. The second most popular is the Bingo, or five-by-five, grid because it is instantly recognizable by the player. See the blank grids at the end of this game.

- For younger students:

  - Present picture clues and have players select the appropriate letter or word on the game sheet.

- Use a game sheet with one letter in each square and ask students to associate words with the letters.

- Use the game to reinforce lowercase letter recognition. Hold up a capital letter ("A," for example) and have students locate the lowercase version ("a").

- For older students:

  - Use a game sheet with a word or short description in each square and ask for association with an item, clue, or definition.

  - Put a "Not Here" square on the game sheet. Tell players that the response for one of the questions may not be found on the game sheet.

  - Use the more competitive *head-to-head* version shown near the end of this game, involving two teams playing one game sheet. This is especially effective in reinforcing material already covered.

Scoring

- If time of play expires with no winners:

  - Assign a value for each square covered, such as 5 points. Have teams tally the total number of squares covered for their final scores.

  - Declare the team with the *most* squares covered to be the winner.

HEAD-TO-HEAD LETTER BINGO

Game Objective   To win by covering 3 or 4 game board squares in a row.

Supplies

- A set of questions and clues about the topic.

- 1 game sheet per set of 2 teams.

- 1 marker per team.

GAME STEPS

Preliminaries

- Divide players into sets of two teams of two or three players each.

- Distribute one game sheet per set of teams.

- Distribute one set of two markers to each set of teams. The two markers must be different from each other.

- Distribute paper and pencils to each team.

- Have each team select an identifying symbol.

Round 1

- Present the first clue.

- Each team races to place its marker on the game sheet.

- When one team covers a square, the other team must select a different square or simply not place its marker on the game sheet.

- Announce the correct response.

Scoring

For a *correct* response, the team marking that response removes its marker *and* writes its symbol in the correct square

For an *incorrect* response, the team marking that response removes its marker from the game sheet

This completes the first round of play.

Round 2 to End of Game

Play is the same for each round.

End of Game

The first team to cover three or four squares in a row with its symbol is declared the winner.

Letter Bingo

B	O	K	H
E	D	J	P
M	I	F	C
G	N	L	A

BLANK GAME SHEET (3 X 3)

Letter Bingo

BLANK GAME SHEET (4 X 4)

Letter Bingo

BLANK GAME SHEET (5 X 5)

Letter Bingo

Letter Bingo

- Divide into teams of two or three.

- Each team receives a game sheet.

- When the first clue is presented, your team places its marker on the letter that represents the correct response.

- Scoring proceeds this way:

  For a *correct* response, your team removes its marker *and* places an "X" through the letter.

  For an *incorrect* response, your team removes its marker.

- Play continues until one team "gets Bingo" by covering four squares in a row.

BINGO 2: MATH BINGO

INTRODUCTION

Math Bingo can enliven data review and give confidence to children who have difficulties with numerical material. Each team receives a Bingo-style game sheet with one or more numbers in each square. As the teacher presents mathematical problems or clues to numerical facts (this is a great way to review statistical information), teams select the numbers they think are the correct answers. The first team to cover four squares correctly in a vertical, horizontal, or corner-to-corner diagonal row wins.

This game, the score cards and blank cards, and the variations presented are adapted from *Framegames by Thiagi*, 7th Edition, by S. Thiagarajan. See other games and ideas by Thiagarajan on his Web site, www.thiagi@thiagi.com.

Purpose	• To strengthen numerical problem-solving skills.
	• To reinforce memorization of abstract data.

Game Objective	To win by covering 4 game board squares in a row.

Players	4 or more. *Can be adapted for one-on-one tutoring.*

Time	15–45 minutes.

Grades	K–8.

Supplies	• A set of clues or numerical problems prepared by the teacher.
	• 1 game sheet per player or team.
	• 1 marker (coin or chip) per team.
	• Paper and pencils for each team.

GAME STEPS

Preliminaries	• Divide class into teams of two or three players each.
	• Distribute one game sheet and marker to each team.

Round 1	• Present the first word or picture clue.
	• Each team places its marker on the game sheet number or numbers representing the correct response.
	• Announce the correct response.

Scoring	For a *correct* response, the team removes its marker *and* marks an "X" through that square.

Scoring   For a *correct* response, the team removes its marker *and* marks an "X" through that square.

For an *incorrect* response, the teams removes its marker from the game sheet.

This completes the first round of play.

Round 2 to End of Game

Play is the same for each round.

End of Game   The first team to cover four squares in a row is declared the winner.

SCORING EXAMPLE

Preliminaries
- The class is divided into teams of two to three players.
- Each team receives a game sheet:

8	12	4	7
2	5	10	3
13	15	14	11
9	1	6	16

- Students are instructed to find the number that is suggested by the clue.

Round 1

- The teacher reads the first clue: "The sum of $7 + 3 - 5 = ?$"

- Team A thinks "5," and places its marker on the "5":

8	12	4	7
2	⑤	10	3
13	15	14	11
9	1	6	16

- The teacher calls time and gives the correct response: "5."

- The teacher elaborates: "The sum of $7 + 3 = 10$. When you subtract 5 the answer is 5."

- All players remove their markers from the game sheets.

- Those teams who correctly selected "5" cross out that square.

- Team A crosses off the "5" square:

8	12	4	7
2	⌧	10	3
13	15	14	11
9	1	6	16

Round 2

- The teacher reads the second clue: "This is the number of Supreme Court Justices, including the Chief Justice."

- Team A thinks "11," and places its marker on "11":

8	12	4	7
2	⌧	10	3
13	15	14	⑪
9	1	6	16

- The teacher calls time and gives the correct response: "Nine. There are 8 Associate Justices and 1 Chief Justice for a total of 9."

- All players remove their markers from the game sheets.

- The teams who correctly selected "9" cross out that square.

- Because Team A's response was incorrect, its game sheet remains unchanged after Round 2:

8	12	4	7
2	5̶	10	3
13	15	14	11
9	1	6	16

TEACHER NOTES

- This game makes reviewing data, especially critical math procedures, a fun event rather than a task. Math Bingo is especially helpful when reviewing critical information for criterion testing or critical thinking.

- Try this game as a way to spur interest in algebra, geometry, trigonometry, and statistics.

- By placing students in teams of two or three, you may be able to reduce their anxiety of performing *on demand,* especially in large groups. By placing the child in a team that will work with and support the child, you may be able to ease this child into working or presenting in front of a larger group.

- Pair shy students with kind, encouraging teammates. This will boost the shy student's confidence.

- Follow up a math homework assignment with this game. It will demonstrate which procedures were understood and *not* understood in the assignment.

- Reinforce abstract numerical data with this game, such as the number of states in the United States or the number of Supreme Court Justices or the number of a specific amendment in the Bill of Rights.

- This is a hands-on learning experience. The team hears or sees the problem statement, comes up with its response, and searches the game sheet for that response.

- Use this game as another way to involve children who may be having a hard time with the concept of numbers or numerical data. Because of its involvement with different ways of communicating (visual, oral, kinesthetic), the game appeals to learners with different learning styles.

- With grade-appropriate problem statements, this game can be used with any age group:

  - K–1: Reinforce number recognition. Present pictures that show varying numbers of objects, or simply call out a number. Then have the teams select the correct number on their game sheet.

  - 1–2: Present math problems requiring simple addition or subtraction.

  - 3–4: Present multiplication and division problems.

  - Older students: Review basic multiplication and division skills. Focus on word problems that involve a numerical answer. Ask questions about geometry, such as the number of sides of a square, number of degrees in a right angle, and the like.

- The recommended team size is two to three players. You will find that teams larger than this have problems coordinating the decision making and square selection in the time required.

- In a *self-scoring* game, cheating or the appearance of cheating may become an issue. If a team's players are accused of giving themselves a square they did not earn, the teacher should deflect the focus from the team involved and invoke a discussion on *fair play*. Discussion questions such as, "would you do *anything* to win?" or, "what if you saw someone cheating or stealing?" might become the most important learning moment of the game.

- If several teams win simultaneously, consider using game sheets that present the same numbers shown here in differing arrangements, to stagger the scoring.

- Individualize your own game sheets by filling in copies of the blank game sheets found at the end of "Letter Bingo" (the previous game).

- Make sure you have extra game sheets in case children make an error by crossing out the wrong square.

- If the game becomes popular with your students, use it frequently throughout the year.

CUSTOMIZING MATH BINGO

Size of Group
- For one player: Establish a standard time. Challenge the student to cover as many squares as possible on the game sheet within that time.

- For larger groups: Consider placing clues on the chalkboard or use an overhead projector.

Time of Play
- Shorten or lengthen the time of each round in relation to the difficulty of the problem.

- Shorten the game to marking off three squares in a row.

Focus of the Task
- Create variations of the four-by-four grid. The most popular is the Tic-Tac-Toe, or three-by-three, grid because it plays more quickly and is easier to complete. The second most popular is the Bingo, or five-by-five grid, because it is instantly recognizable by the player.

- For younger students: Present picture clues, and ask students to select the number of items in the picture, placing their markers on a "2" in response to a picture showing two apples, for example.

- For older students:

  - Put a "Not Here" square on the game sheet. Tell the players that the response for one of the problems may not be found on the game sheet.

  - Introduce the more competitive *head-to-head* version of Math Bingo, which involves two teams playing one game sheet. This game is most effective when used to reinforce material already covered. See the complete rules of play at the end of this game.

Scoring

If the time of play expires with no winners, declare the team with the *most* squares covered to be the winner.

HEAD-TO-HEAD MATH BINGO

Game Objective

To win by covering 3 or 4 game sheet squares in a row.

Supplies

- A set of questions and clues about the topic.

- 1 game sheet per set of 2 teams.

- 1 marker per team.

Game Steps

- Divide players into sets of two teams of two or three players each.

- Distribute one game sheet per set of teams.

- Distribute one set of two markers to each set of teams. The two markers must be different from each other.

- Distribute paper and pencils to each team.

- Have each team select an identifying symbol.

Round 1

- Read the first problem statement.

- Each team races to place its marker on the game sheet.

- When one team covers a square, the other team must select a different square or simply not place its marker on the game sheet.

- Announce the correct response.

Scoring

For a *correct* response, the team marking that response removes its marker *and* writes its symbol in the correct square

For an *incorrect* response, the team marking that response removes its marker from the game sheet

This completes the first round of play.

Round 2 to End of Game

Play is the same for each round.

End of Game

The first team to cover three or four squares in a row is declared the winner.

Math Bingo

8	12	4	7
2	5	10	3
13	15	14	11
9	1	6	16

- Divide into teams of two or three.

- Each team receives a game sheet.

- The teacher presents a clue.

- Your team places its marker on the number that represents the correct response.

- Scoring is as follows:

    For a *correct* response, your team removes its marker *and* places an "X" through the number.

    For an *incorrect* response, your team removes its marker.

- Play continues until one team "gets Bingo" by covering four squares in a row.

BINGO 3: WALL BINGO

INTRODUCTION   Wall Bingo, a fast-paced game played by two or three teams on a large Bingo-style game sheet placed on the wall, may remind students of the TV game show, *Jeopardy.* Teams select the number of points they want to try for and get a question appropriate to that point level. If the team's response is correct, the teacher covers the square and awards the team the designated points. Teams also get bonus points for covering three or more squares in a row. This is an excellent game for tutoring small groups of students in a variety of topics.

Purpose	• To review a variety of information in a challenging format.
	• To learn about group decision making.

Game Objective	To collect the most team points.

Players	2 or more. *Can be adapted for one-on-one tutoring.*

Time	20–45 minutes.

Grades	3–8.

Supplies	• Sets of questions on 2 to 4 topics, prepared in advance by the teacher.
	• 1 large-sized game sheet.
	• Set of Post-Its or masking tape and index cards (square covers).
	• Paper and pencils for players.

GAME STEPS

Preliminaries	• Make the wall game sheet. Determine the number of topics (from two to four), and then draw your wall game grid on an oversize sheet of newsprint paper with felt-tipped markers, filling in column heads and point values. Follow the sample game sheets at the end of the chapter.
	• Prepare the question sets. Prepare twelve or more questions for each topic *column* on your game sheet.

- Two topics (four columns) = 24 questions for each topic.

- Three topics = 17 questions for each topic (an extra 5 questions for the *mixed* topic column).

- Four topics = 12 questions for each topic.

- Make the square *covers* showing the team names. You place a cover on the appropriate game square when a team responds correctly to a question. Create the covers from index cards, which can be stuck to the wall sheet squares with masking tape, or self-sticking paper, such as Post-It notes. A square cover removes that square from play and later indicates the scores to be tallied for each team. You should provide at least eight square covers for each team.

- Divide the class into two or three teams.

Round 1: Team A
- Team A selects a square showing a particular point value on the game sheet.

- Temporarily cover the square, and then ask a question.

Scoring

For a *correct* response, award Team A the appropriate points and put the Team A square cover over the square.

For an *incorrect* response, award 0 points and uncover the square.

Play then moves to the next team.

Round 2 to End of Game

All rounds are played in the same fashion.

End of Game
The team with the most points is declared the winner.

SCORING EXAMPLE

Preliminaries
- The class is divided into two teams: Team A and Team B.

- The teacher has prepared a game sheet with two topics in math and spelling.

- Team A responds first.

Round 1: Team A

- Team A selects a 20-point question in math.

- The teacher temporarily covers the square and presents the question.

Math	Spelling	Math	Spelling
10	10	10	10
20	20	20	20
30	30	30	30
40	40	40	40

- Team A responds correctly to the question.

- The teacher awards 20 points to Team A and covers the square with a paper showing the words "Team A."

Math	Spelling	Math	Spelling
10	10	10	10
Team A	20	20	20
30	30	30	30
40	40	40	40

Round 1: Team B

- Team B selects a 20-point question in spelling.

- The teacher temporarily covers the square and presents the question.

Math	Spelling	Math	Spelling
10	10	10	10
Team A	20	20	20
30	30	30	30
40	40	40	40

- Team B responds incorrectly to the question.

- Team B receives 0 points, and the teacher uncovers the square.

Math	Spelling	Math	Spelling
10	10	10	10
Team A	20	20	20
30	30	30	30
40	40	40	40

- This completes Round 1.

- Round 1 Scores: Team A = 20 points, Team B = 0 points.

Round 2: Team A

- Team A selects a 30-point question in math.

- The teacher temporarily covers the square and presents a question.

Math	Spelling	Math	Spelling
10	10	10	10
Team A	20	20	20
→ 30	30	30	30
40	40	40	40

- Team A responds correctly to the question.

- The teacher awards 30 points to Team A and covers the square with "Team A."

Math	Spelling	Math	Spelling
10	10	10	10
Team A	20	20	20
Team A	30	30	30
40	40	40	40

- Score: Team A = 20 + 30 = 50 points.

Round 2: Team B

- Team B selects a 40-point question in math.

- The teacher temporarily covers the square and presents the question.

Math	Spelling	Math	Spelling
10	10	10	10
Team A	20	20	20
Team A	30	30	30
→40	40	40	40

- Team B responds correctly to the question.

- The teacher awards 40 points to Team B *and* covers the square with "Team B."

Math	Spelling	Math	Spelling
10	10	10	10
Team A	20	20	20
Team A	30	30	30
Team B	40	40	40

- This completes Round 2.

- Score: Team A = 50 points, Team B = 40 points.

- *Scoring note:* Consider awarding a bonus of 50 points for any team covering three squares in a row and 100 points for any team covering four squares in a row.

TEACHER NOTES

- What a wonderful way to create a television quiz show atmosphere in your own classroom. The excitement and mystery of seeing a large Bingo sheet on the wall will remind most students of the popular quiz program *Jeopardy,* but with rules and a setup that make it easier for you to prepare and control play.

- Use this game to bring an excellent mix of game play and subject recall to tutoring sessions of two or three students. The fast pace of the game will make a session that is usually a little slow, such as afternoon tutoring, an anticipated event.

- Use this game as a whole class game. Ask the students how they plan to involve everyone in the decision-making process when coming up with an answer. Here are some suggestions:

  - Have the team collaborate, and then have a team spokesperson give the response.

  - Allow the student who is most sure of his answer give the response.

- Have team players take turns giving the response.

- Have each team line up in single file and then select the first player in line to respond to the next question. After taking a turn, the player goes to the end of the line.

- Have one player from the team whose turn it is walk to the wall chart and select a square. This gets players out of their chairs and adds variety.

- Use partial scoring, awarding a portion of a score for a partially correct response. Players feel much better when they know that their response was almost correct or just a little off the mark. Awarding partial scores overcomes players' anxiety about having to give perfect responses and encourages players to take a chance even if they feel they may not be completely correct.

- For younger groups:

  - Read the questions aloud.

  - Use a picture to clarify each question.

  - Use the scoring at the end of each round to reinforce counting.

  - Have the players keep their own scores and then compare them with your own tally.

  - Number the squares to reflect curriculum topics, using Roman numerals, higher number combinations (100, 200, 300), and the like.

- This game is suitable for home schooling different aged children. Let the children play against each other, no matter their level, by using questions suitable to the answering student or team. This allows everyone to compete yet still provides a fair challenge to each level.

- By using temporary stick-on notes, such as Post-It notes, you can reuse the same wall game sheet over and over again.

- Create an overhead transparency of the game sheet and play the game using the overhead projector.

- Use a *secret bonus* square. Select one or two squares on the wall chart to be bonus squares. When a team answers a question for this square correctly, the team receives a bonus of additional points or continued play. The secret square is eligible for only one turn—if the team that selects the square does not respond correctly, no one receives the bonus.

- Use a noisemaker, such as a call bell, to announce when a round is complete, a team has given a correct response, or a team is eligible for a bonus (covering three or four squares in a row).

- Invite each team to help you tally their points. What better way to involve students in real-life math skills while assuring each team that they receive an accurate point total? This tactic is especially helpful when counting bonus points.

- You may find it helpful to use one or more student assistants to help you track the time and score and to maintain the game board. This can help you focus on presenting the questions, qualifying the correct responses, and awarding points. You will find that students enjoy the real-time experience as "score keeper," "time keeper," and "keeper of the (game) board."

- Prepare two or more questions for each square. Extra questions can always be used in "miscellaneous" categories or as tiebreakers.

- Prepare each set of topic questions on separately marked "topic" sheets.

  - Write the questions at two or three levels of difficulty, with the more challenging questions on the bottom of the sheet.

  - Color-code each "topic" sheet to correspond with the topic it represents on the game sheet. When a team indicates a topic and point value, confirm the selected topic's color, and level of difficulty, with your color-coded sheet.

  - Cross off each question as you present it. This eliminates confusion over which question has already been presented.

- As you present the questions, make a note of which question(s) seemed particularly difficult to your class. You may want to review this material later within your lecture or readings. You may also consider re-stating this question later in the game.

- Prepare three sets of ten index cards with the letters A, B, and C. Create each set of ten cards on different colored cardstock and then trim them to fit into the space on the game sheet. The letter-and-color cards help teams track their spaces while simplifying your task of tabulating the point total.

CUSTOMIZING WALL BINGO

Size of Group

- For one player:

Time Driven

- Have player answer as many questions as she can in a two-minute period.

- Establish a standard and a best score to serve as a scoring range for the single player.

Quantity Driven

- Have player answer as many questions as he can before giving an incorrect response.

- Establish a standard and a best score to serve as a scoring range for the single player.

- For large groups:

- Have one section play the game while the other section watches.

- Review the results of the game with the entire class.

Time of Play
- Set a time limit within which a team must provide a response to a question, such as ten seconds.
- Play for a specific length of time or number of rounds.
- Play a continuing game of two or three rounds a day for an entire week. Maintain interest in the scores by posting them on the bulletin board.

Focus of the Task
- Have a different player represent a team in each round. Play enough rounds that everyone has a chance to respond to a question.
- Have teams compete to be the first to respond to a question. Give each team a different noisemaker and then present the question. The first team to sound its noisemaker responds to the question.
- If a team misses a question, allow other teams to respond and receive the point value of the square.
- Assign each team a topic, and challenge teams to *run the topic* by responding correctly to each question in the topic column. Each team stops after its first wrong response.
- Create game sheets with five squares in each column to reflect *Jeopardy* more closely.
- Increase the difficulty of questions to reflect the risk of selecting questions with higher point values.

Scoring
- Bonus Scoring:
  - Award 50 points when a team covers three squares in a row (vertically, horizontally, or corner-to-corner).
  - Award 100 points when a team covers four squares in a row (vertically, horizontally, or corner-to-corner).
  - Increase the point values of the squares to 100, 200, 300, and 400 points.

- Award partial scores, such as half the point value, for partially correct or almost acceptable responses, to reinforce a "less than perfect is still OK" class atmosphere.

- Conduct "risk" rounds where points are deducted for incorrect responses.

Wall Bingo (2-Topic)

Select two topics to be placed along the X-axis as the column heads.
Alternate the topics: Topic 1, Topic 2, Topic 1, and Topic 2.
Place a question point value inside each square.

Topic 1	Topic 2	Topic 1	Topic 2
10	10	10	10
20	20	20	20
30	30	30	30
40	40	40	40

Wall Bingo (3-Topic)

Select three topics to be placed along the X-axis as the column heads.
Place the topics in order: Topic 1, Topic 2, Topic 3. Title the fourth column "Mixed" (a random mix of the three topics).
Place a question point value inside each square.

Topic 1	Topic 2	Topic 3	Mixed
10	10	10	10
20	20	20	20
30	30	30	30
40	40	40	40

Wall Bingo (3-Topic)

Place the point values in an increasing, or ascending, order to visually reinforce the higher values (by putting them higher on the chart).

Topic 1	Topic 2	Topic 3	Mixed
40	40	40	40
30	30	30	30
20	20	20	20
10	10	10	10

Wall Bingo (4-Topic)

Select four topics to be placed along the X-axis as the column heads.
Place the four topics in order: Topic 1, Topic 2, Topic 3, Topic 4.
Place a question point value inside each square.

Topic 1	Topic 2	Topic 3	Topic 4
10	10	10	10
20	20	20	20
30	30	30	30
40	40	40	40

Wall Bingo

Round	Team	Team	Team
1			
2			
3			
4			
5			
Bonus Points			
Total Points			

- Form two or three teams.

- The first team selects a square showing a point value.

- The teacher presents a question.

- Scoring follows this pattern:

   For a *correct* response, the team earns the appropriate points and the team cover is placed over the square.

   For an *incorrect* response, the team earns 0 points.

- Play moves to the next team.

- After all rounds have been played, the team with the most points wins.

BITS AND PIECES

INTRODUCTION   In Bits and Pieces, each player has one piece of a cut-up shape, with part of an academic task written on it, and must exercise shape and pattern recognition skills to find other players whose pieces complete the shape and the description of the task. The players whose pieces fit together must then form an effective team, working together to complete the task written on the shape. Problem-solving and teamwork skills get a workout in this game, which is a good choice when children are returning to the classroom after a long weekend and need to be refocused on their work.

This game, originally created as an icebreaker activity for *Games That Teach*, by Steve Sugar, has been reformatted for this audience.

| **Purpose** | • To cultivate problem-solving skills. |
| | • To develop shape and pattern recognition abilities. |

Game Objective   To complete the task revealed by the completed shape.

Players   4 or more. *Can be adapted for one-on-one tutoring.*

Time   15–30 minutes.

Grades   K–8.

Supplies
- A set of task assignments, prepared in advance by the facilitator.
- 3 or more sheets of construction paper in various colors.
- 2 or more fine-tipped permanent markers.
- Scissors or paper cutter.
- 4 or more envelopes.
- Paper and pencils for the students.

GAME STEPS

Preliminaries
- Determine the number of students you will have in each task group.
- Determine the number of task assignments you will need to have one task for each group of students. Tasks might ask students to prepare a list of certain things.
- Select a shape for each task, and then draw each shape on a sheet of construction paper. For larger classes you may have to repeat this procedure, drawing the same shape on two or more *different* colors of construction paper.

- For each task, write different parts of the task on different parts of the shape. Then cut the shape into the appropriate number of irregular pieces. For example, if you want four players in each group and one of the shapes you have made is a circle on red construction paper, cut this red circle into four irregular pieces, each piece showing a portion of the task. (See the sample game sheet at the end of this game.)

- Store each cut-up shape in its own envelope.

- When you are ready to play the game, set up a working area equipped with paper and pencils for *each* team.

A Complete Game

- Have students assemble in an open area of the room.

- Hand out one piece of a shape to each student. (If there are absentees, you may need to give some players two puzzle pieces instead of one.)

- Tell players to find others with pieces of the same shape (and color if the same shapes appear in different colors).

- Have the players in each group assemble their shape at one of the working areas.

- Make sure that each newly formed team understands its task.

- Give each team five minutes to complete its task.

- At the end of five minutes, have each team report on its task.

Scoring

Scoring is optional. If you use it:

Each item developed in response to a task = 1 point

End of Game

Optional close: The team with the most points is declared the winner.

TEACHER NOTES

- This is an excellent activity to get children working collaboratively in a group and generating ideas about a topic. This reinforces their understanding of the topic and ability to apply it.

- Problem solving is a difficult skill to teach. The random formation of the task group and the pressure to develop solutions gives students problem-solving experience and allows you to test their skills.

- Use this game when you have tasks in mind that require listing items from the curriculum.

- Use shapes without tasks to give students experience with forming and working in random teams. Later, once the students are familiar with the process of the game and team formation, the shapes can be *loaded* with tasks corresponding to the curriculum.

- This game allows students to complete several assignments—from forming teams to the completion of a task—thus underscoring their sense of accomplishment.

- This is a great game for brainstorming. Get each group working on the task and then bring the whole class back together to share thoughts.

- Consider using this game as a constructive way to bring students back into the curriculum following a long weekend or vacation. The immediacy of the task creates classroom energy and a focus on the topic at hand.

- Conduct a *scavenger hunt* by using the completed task assignments as clues in a search for "classroom items." These items may be related to the lesson material (for example: list objects in the classroom that start with the letter "C").

- For younger groups:

  - Distribute pieces of the shape without written tasks. This will familiarize children with both the shape and the color used.

- Make shapes from cut-up photocopies of the front covers of books you have been reading in the classroom. The pictures, and later the words, will act as clues to help young players assemble the shape. (Mount the picture first on a manila folder or heavy construction paper, then cut it into shapes. Laminate for continued use.)

- For slightly advanced younger groups: Distribute pieces of the shape with one- or two-word tasks or a simple math problem. Have them solve these simple problems.

- For older groups: Create tasks taken from the curriculum or have the students create their own tasks. Tasks created by students often reflect their perception of what is important about the topic. Rather than choosing specific tasks from these student efforts, you might select tasks randomly.

CUSTOMIZING BITS AND PIECES

Size of Group

- For one player:

  - In a race against a five-minute game time, the player receives one piece of the shape each time she responds correctly to a preliminary question.

  - Once she assembles the shape, she can begin the task.

- For larger groups:

  - Prepare shapes in several colors but containing the same task. Have the teams prepare their lists separately in response to their tasks, and then have the teams present their findings separately *or* have all teams with the same task meet together to share and compare their findings.

  - Split the class into sections. Have one section form teams, complete their tasks, and present their lists as the other section watches. Review the results of the game with the entire class.

- When using at least two sets of shapes in two or more colors, have an overall task for the collected teams working with each shape. For example, an orange circle team, a yellow circle team, a blue circle team, and a green circle team might combine to perform the circle shape's task. They might compete against the teams assembling squares to be the first to complete a task.

Time of Play

Allow more or less time, depending on the complexity of the task assignments or the age level of the students.

Focus of the Task

- For older groups:

    - Omit one piece from each shape to give students practice in dealing with ambiguity and critical thinking.

    - Identify which students took which roles in the completion of the task. This can lead to a discussion of leadership and how to work in a team.

    - Switch task assignments immediately after each team has completed its list, but before the teams have reported. Each team now gets to expand on the original solutions devised by another team.

    - Allow students to use reference materials to complete the task assignment.

- For younger players: Number the sections of the shapes. After players form the appropriate teams, discuss the similarities and differences of the shapes.

Scoring

- Award a 3-point bonus to the first team to complete its task assignment.

- Have the students in the class vote for their favorite solutions.

Bits and Pieces

Shape selected: circle

Number of group members: 4

Grade: 5

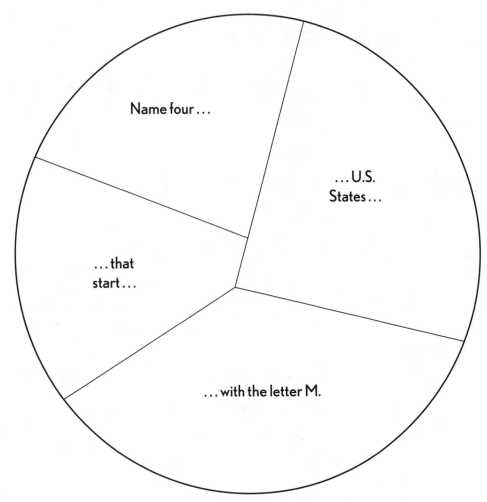

Bits and Pieces

- Receive one piece of a shape.

- Find other players with pieces of the same shape and form a team.

- Complete the task written on the completed shape.

- Report on your completed task.

BUBBLES

INTRODUCTION
In the game of Bubbles a correct response to a question earns three blows on a bubble maker and even incorrect answers earn one blow. A team receives 1 point for each bubble counted. The questions can review any topic, the processes of blowing bubbles and scoring can be tied to practical math and science lessons, and the game can offer many levels of involvement.

| **Purpose** | • To increase understanding and ability to apply information. |
| | • To energize through competition while fostering participation. |

| **Game Objective** | To score the most points. |

| **Players** | 4 or more. *Can be adapted for one-on-one tutoring.* |

| **Time** | 15–35 minutes. |

| **Grades** | K–5. |

Supplies	• A set of questions, developed in advance by the teacher.
	• 2 or more bottles of soapy solution and a bubble maker.
	• Paper and pencils.
	• Wipe cloths or paper towels.
	• A large sheet or drop cloth (optional).

GAME STEPS

| **Preliminaries** | • Divide class into two or three teams. |

| **Round 1** | • Present the first question. |
| | • Give the team fifteen seconds to respond. |

Scoring	A *correct* response = 3 blows on the bubble maker
	An *incorrect* response = 1 blow on the bubble maker
	No response = 0 blows on the bubble maker

- Have Team A count the number of bubbles made by the bubble maker.
- Award 1 point for each bubble.
- Record Team A's score on the chalkboard.

Round 2 to End of Game

- All rounds are played in the same manner.

End of Game
- The team with the most points is declared the winner.

SCORING EXAMPLE

Preliminaries
- The class is divided into three teams—Team A, Team B, and Team C.

Round 1: Team A
- The teacher presents the first question.
- Team A has fifteen seconds to respond.
- Team A responds correctly within fifteen seconds.
- The teacher awards Team A three blows on the bubble maker.
- A Team A player blows three times on the bubble maker.
- Team A counts thirty-six bubbles, and the teacher records 36 points.
- Play moves on to Team B.

Round 1: Team B
- The teacher presents the second question.
- Team B responds incorrectly within fifteen seconds.
- The teacher awards Team B one blow on the bubble maker.

- A Team B player blows one time on the bubble maker.

- Team B counts fourteen bubbles, and the teacher records 14 points.

- Play moves on to Team C.

Round 1: Team C

- The teacher presents the third question.

- Team C fails to respond within the fifteen-second period.

- The teacher does not give Team C any blows on the bubble maker.

- The teacher records 0 points.

- This completes play for Round 1.

Scoring for Round 1

Team A: 3 blows for a total of 36 points

Team B: 1 blow for a total of 14 points

Team C: 0 blows for a total of 0 points

TEACHER NOTES

- *Caution:* Be careful of slippery floor surfaces, especially on tile floors. Warn the children not to run during and following the game until you can wipe up any bubble solution. If you are concerned about bubbles and slippery floors:

  - Change the reward format to *basket tosses* using wadded paper balls. See the notes about scoring in the section on customizing this game.

  - Use a drop cloth or take the game outdoors.

- Bubbles are such fun that this game is a particular favorite with children at the elementary level.

- Awarding one turn on the bubble maker for an incorrect response encourages children, especially the younger ones, to attempt a response. Participating in large groups may cause children to be timid or unsure of their answers. This award underscores that trying, even when you are not sure, is better than not trying at all.

- The bubble count can be made by . . .

  - The teacher or teacher's assistant.

  - Preselected *Bubble Police.*

  - Students selected as *Star of the Week.*

  - Student or students whose birthdays fall during the week of the game.

  - Each team (each player on the team makes a count and these counts are then averaged for the final count for the round for that team). This method can be used with older students as a practical introduction to statistics and math.

- Have the children observe the bubbles and estimate how long it took for the bubbles to pop or land on the floor or other objects. This can tie in with a lesson on seconds and minutes as time components.

- Use the action of soap bubbles to discuss concepts of gravity, floating objects, and what a bubble is.

- Have each team select a *Bubble Master,* the person who blows on the bubble maker to create the bubbles.

- This game can be used with all ages, even nonreaders, because the questions are given verbally.

- Older students can play this game at a learning center.

CUSTOMIZING BUBBLES

Size of Group

- For one or two players:

  - Let the student set a goal for how many bubbles he will get to blow for answering five questions.

  - Establish a standard number of bubbles. Challenge the student to match or better the score within a stated or open time period.

- For larger groups: Have half the class practice blowing bubbles with a teaching assistant outside while the other half is playing. Then have the two groups switch places.

- For younger groups: Make the teams smaller. This makes it easier for teams to agree on one response and shortens the time between the response and the bubble blowing.

Time of Play

- Lengthen the time of the question response period to thirty seconds or even one minute, depending on the difficulty of the question or the attention span of the students.

- Use the bubbles as a timer—ask a question and then blow a series of bubbles. The team must deliver its response before the first bubble pops.

Focus of the Task

- Present questions requiring several responses. Award one blow for each five responses.

- Require teams to solve a problem statement. Award one blow for each correct response.

Scoring

- Introduce special questions that are worth extra blows on the bubble maker.

- Change the reward system to *basket tosses*. Set up a trash can and have several wadded paper balls available. When a team responds correctly, its players get five tosses at the basket. When a team misses the question, players get two tosses. The team gets no tosses when no team members respond. Count each basket the team makes as 1 point.

Bubbles

Round	Team	Team	Team
1	_____ Bubble blows _____ Points	_____ Bubble blows _____ Points	_____ Bubble blows _____ Points
2	_____ Bubble blows _____ Points	_____ Bubble blows _____ Points	_____ Bubble blows _____ Points
3	_____ Bubble blows _____ Points	_____ Bubble blows _____ Points	_____ Bubble blows _____ Points
4	_____ Bubble blows _____ Points	_____ Bubble blows _____ Points	_____ Bubble blows _____ Points
5	_____ Bubble blows _____ Points	_____ Bubble blows _____ Points	_____ Bubble blows _____ Points
Total Points			

- Form two or three teams.

- The teacher presents a question to the first team.

- Scoring is as follows:

> A *correct* response = 3 blows on the bubble maker
>
> An *incorrect* response = 1 blow on the bubble maker
>
> *No* response = 0 blows on the bubble maker

- Receive 1 point for each bubble.

CROSSWORDS

INTRODUCTION   Crosswords can be used in place of worksheets to review concepts and vocabulary and to get students used to looking up what they don't know. This game can also accustom students to contributing to team efforts. Each player receives a game sheet (a grid with numbers matching the clue numbers) and a clue sheet and then works both individually and with the other players on his team. Each team must solve as many items on the game sheet as it can within the prescribed time. This game is also great as a take-home assignment, and completed game sheets can be kept as test study guides.

Purpose	• To reinforce course terminology or content.
	• To promote critical thinking and problem solving.
	• To promote team cooperation and sharing.

| **Game Objective** | To solve as many clues as possible, placing the correct word or words on the crossword game sheet. |

| **Players** | 1 or more. *Can be adapted for one-on-one tutoring.* |

| **Time** | 20–45 minutes. |

| **Grades** | 3–8. |

| **Supplies** | • 1 puzzle game sheet and 1 clue sheet for each player. |
| | • References, notes, or handout materials, as necessary. |

GAME STEPS

Preliminaries	• Develop a list of important concepts or key words for your topic.
	• Draw a game sheet manually or with a software program. See the sample game sheet at the end of this game. Your blank game sheet will not contain the answers, but it will contain the numbers that match up with your clue sheet.
	• Develop the list of clues.

A Complete Game	• Divide the class into two to five teams.
	• Distribute one game sheet and one clue sheet to each student.
	• Instruct the teams that they have twenty minutes to complete as many of the items as they can.

- Optional: Inform teams that they may refer to their readings and notes.

- Call time at the end of twenty minutes.

- Go over the game sheet with the class.

- The team with the largest number of correct items wins.

TEACHER NOTES

- The crossword puzzle as we know it today was first published on December 21, 1913, in the *New York World*. The creator, Arthur Wynne, devised it to fill space in the entertainment section, calling it "Word-Cross." For almost a century, the crossword has been one of the most popular types of puzzles for children and adults alike.

- This game generates excitement for and brings teamwork to an activity often used only in the form of a seatwork worksheet. It brings new life to what could be a tedious task for some students. Letting children work together and adding a friendly competitive dimension to a simple crossword puzzle allows students to think in a different way than usual and to feel the excitement of competition.

- You can create a simple puzzle by manually laying out the word solutions on graph paper. Duplicate your puzzle on a copy of the grid worksheet provided at the end of this game, or use a spreadsheet and analysis program with a graphing and charting function, such as Excel.

- Consider using crossword puzzles throughout the school year to review important vocabulary or concepts.

- Younger grades (3–6) may not be able to sit down to a crossword puzzle for fifteen minutes. If your students are getting fidgety, then call time sooner than fifteen minutes. Inform the groups they have three more minutes to finish the puzzle. This will get them back on track and help you with classroom management.

- Encourage students to use any reference materials they wish, establishing a friendly open-book environment.

- Encourage students to keep their completed puzzle sheets for future reference.

- Hand out this game a few days before a test on the materials covered so your students can use the clue sheet and finished crossword as a study guide. This is a fun way to get students into productive study habits.

- Give out *completed* game sheets, and have your students construct clues for each solution shown. Allow students to refer to homework and other reference materials.

- When going over the correct solutions, place a game sheet on an overhead, and solicit one solution at a time from different teams. This review gives your students an opportunity to see how other players solved each clue.

- Once you have introduced the crossword puzzle to the students, consider varying when and how it is played:

  - Play Crosswords individually or in teams.

  - Play in class or as a take-home exercise.

  - Play in a fixed time period—the team with the highest number of correct answers wins.

  - Play to completion—the first team to complete the puzzle wins.

  - Break a puzzle into two segments, and then have teams trade clues with their opponents. Team A receives a puzzle sheet with only "across" solutions; Team B receives a puzzle sheet with only "down" solutions. Teams prepare a clue for each solution and then share these clues on alternate turns—Team A offers a clue to "1 Across," and then Team B offers a clue to "1 Down," and so on. This process is repeated until all clues are shared between the two teams.

  - Play Crosswords as an ongoing exercise in tandem with the current study module.

- Use the *think-pair-share* technique. Allow your students to think about and work on a puzzle alone for ten minutes before pairing (getting together in their groups) and then sharing. This allows students to gather their thoughts and come up with original ideas before combining with the group, making the group time more productive.

- For foreign language training:

  - State clues in the foreign language but require solutions in English.

  - State clues in English but require solutions in the foreign language.

- For younger students:

  - Use clues of simple word groups and pictures. As they grow accustomed to the game and their skills increase, increase the difficulty of the clues.

  - Puzzle clues may be presented in written form or as pictures shown on the overhead or held up in front of the class.

- For older students:

  - Have them write clues for the puzzles. It will give you a view of what they think is important and will help you write student-friendly puzzle clues.

  - Give them portions of a completed puzzle and have them form teams and create new clues. Then have the teams trade and share these clues with other teams.

- Clues for the crossword can be written to *any* level of understanding, allowing you to customize the puzzle for your class and topic. Try this for yourself: create clues at four different levels for one of your game sheet answers.

- Consult www.thiagi@thiagi.com for further ideas about creating and using crossword puzzles or other types of puzzles in your classroom.

CUSTOMIZING CROSSWORDS

Size of Group

- For one player:

  - Fixed time: Have the player identify as many items as possible.

  - Open time: Have the player complete an entire game sheet.

- For small groups: Divide into two teams and have them compete against each other for a specified time.

Time of Play

- Vary the time according to the grade level and topic.

- Use the puzzle as a take-home, self-paced exercise to review old material or to introduce new vocabulary.

- Have teams play to completion of the puzzle; the first team to complete the puzzle wins.

- Begin the puzzle in class, stop play when students are only partly done, and continue play on it the next day. See how many of your students did home research between the two game periods.

Focus of the Task

- Vary the difficulty of the clues according to the level of the players.

- Post an open game sheet and set of clues on the bulletin board, and encourage students to fill in the items during breaks and recess.

- Distribute the puzzles to individual students for take-home completion.

- Use the puzzles as reinforcement for homework assignments.

- Give everyone a puzzle sheet and then present the clues one by one on the overhead, seeking responses to each clue from the students.

- Allow students to refer to text or reference materials.

Scoring

- Award 1 point for each clue solved.

- Award 1 point for each letter of a word that is a solution to a clue.

- Increase the number of points in accordance with the difficulty of the item.

- Award a 10-point bonus for completing the puzzle.

- Suggested ways to determine a team's final score:

  - Collect one game sheet from each team and then tally the teams' scores yourself.

  - Have teams exchange and score each other's game sheets.

  - Have each team tally its own score and report it to the teacher.

Crosswords

Across ⟶

2. Opposite of hard; we use ____ware programs to make our computers run

4. Having a sharp or acid taste; opposite of sweet

5. To keep out of sight; the dog ____ her bones

6. A friend, buddy, or chum

Down

1. Very intense sound, high volume

2. Top layer of earth's surface, suitable for growing plant life

3. When you do not have to pay for an item, you get it for ____.

4. A part of something; belonging to a group

Crosswords

			L				
		S	O	F	T		
		S	O	U	R		
	S	H	I	D	E	S	
	P	A	L		E		
		R					
		E					

Crosswords

- Form into two to five teams.

- Each player receives a game sheet and a clue sheet.

- Each team writes in as many solutions as it can on the game sheet in the time allowed.

- The team that solves the most clues is declared the winner.

DILEMMA

INTRODUCTION Playing Dilemma can improve recognition of similarities and differences among topic items and enhance decision-making abilities. Game sheets naming two or more categories are placed on a wall, and players must sort cards naming various items, placing each card under one of the categories on the game sheet. Although often played as a team game, Dilemma, in a desk version, also makes a good learning center game for individual students.

This game, originally created as a sorting game for *Games That Teach,* by Steve Sugar, has been reformatted for this audience.

Purpose	• To enhance skills in identifying differences and similarities among a set of items.
	• To develop analytical and decision-making abilities.
Game Objective	To score the most team points.
Players	6 or more. *Can be adapted for one-on-one tutoring.*
Time	15–30 minutes.
Grades	K–8.
Supplies	• 2 or more wall game sheets, prepared in advance by the teacher.
	• For each game sheet, 1 set of items written on three-by-five-inch index cards.
	• Masking tape, to attach index cards to game sheets.
	• A stopwatch or other timing device (optional).

GAME STEPS

Preliminaries	• Prepare two or more game wall sheets with category names separated by a vertical line.
	• Post the prepared game sheets on the wall.
	• Place strips of masking tape (for fixing the cards to the game sheet) and one set of cards (face down) on a table near each posted game sheet.
	• Divide the class into two to five teams.
	• Have each team line up in single file in front of its game sheet.

Round 1

- Have the first player from each team pick up, turn over, and read a card and then move to the game sheet and tape the card under the proper category.

  (Note that the next player cannot touch the next card until the previous card is placed on the game sheet.)

- After the first card is placed, have the next player repeat the procedure.

- Continue play in this fashion until time is called.

- Review the cards, and award the appropriate points.

Scoring

A *correctly* placed card = 1 point

An *incorrectly* placed card = 0 points

A card *not played* = 0 points

Round 2 to End of Game

- Play is the same for each round.

End of Game

- The team with the most points is declared the winner.

SCORING EXAMPLE

Preliminaries

- The teacher decides to use this game to reinforce the importance of odd and even numbers and to divide the students into two teams to play the game.

- The teacher prepares two sets of eleven index cards by placing a number on one side of each card.

- The teacher prepares two game sheets by placing the words "Odd" and "Even" at the top of the sheet and drawing a vertical line separating the two categories.

- The teacher places one set of cards *face down* by each of the game sheets, along with strips of masking tape.

| 3 | 14 | 41 | 21 | 10 |

| 9 | 32 | 12 | 7 | 8 | 11 |

Odd	Even

- The class is divided into two teams.

- Each team lines up single file by the set of cards placed near its game sheet.

- The teacher reminds both teams that only the player holding the card can place it on the game sheet and that no one else on the team can place a card until that player has completed his or her turn.

Round 1

- The first player from each team turns over the first card, walks to his team's game sheet, and places the card under one of the two categories.

- Play continues in this fashion until the teacher calls time at the end of one minute.

Scoring: Team A

- Team A placed its cards this way:

  Placed under "Even": 8, 10, 12, 14

  Placed under "Odd": 3, 9, 11, 41

  Not played: 7, 21, 32

- The teacher awards 1 point each for the following correct placements:

Correct placements "Even": 8, 10, 12, 14	= 4 points
Correct placements "Odd": 3, 9, 11, 41	= 4 points
Not played: 7, 21, 32	= 0 points
Total	8 points

- The teacher posts 8 points for Team A.

Scoring: Team B

- Team B placed its cards this way:

  Placed under "Even": 8, 10, 12, 14

  Placed under "Odd": 3, 9, 11, 21, 32, 41

  Not played: 7

- The teacher awards 1 point each for the following correct placements:

Correct placements "Even": 8, 10, 12, 14	= 4 points
Correct placements "Odd": 3, 9, 11, 21, 41	= 5 points
Not played: 7	= 0 points
Total	9 points

- The teacher posts 9 points for Team B.

TEACHER NOTES

- This is an excellent activity for physical game and decision making. Having children choosing and then placing an item into a category shapes the subject matter and makes it more meaningful.

- It is important to vary the instructional format. This game breaks the tell-and-test cycle with an activity that keeps the children up and moving.

- Decision making is a difficult skill for children to learn. By requiring the player to make a *forced choice,* this game can provide a practice environment for learning decision-making skills.

- Create desk versions of the game sheets—drawn on 8.5-by-11-inch paper, with accompanying lists of unsorted items—for individual or small-group play. These desk versions work well as homework assignments, for home schooling one or two students, or as learning center activities. (See the sample game sheet at the end of this game.)

- Countless categories can be used with this game. In addition to the normal curriculum categories, the teacher can set up the game to differentiate among almost any set of items, ranging from prime and not prime among numbers, fruits and vegetables among crops, and appropriate actions and inappropriate actions among behaviors.

- Requiring the children to actively place an item in the correct category will spark many after-game discussions. Children will be actively involved in the material, getting more out of the lesson than they would by just memorizing facts.

- Commission your students to create categories. If appropriate, adopt them for your game.

- Use this game as an excellent vehicle for introducing all levels of math concepts and procedures, ranging from odd and even numbers to Venn diagrams.

- Allow teams to tally their own points to reinforce their math skills.

- For younger students:
    - Use words or pictures to depict the item or to define the column headings on the game sheet.
    - Have players place picture items under the appropriate letter.
- For older students: State that one or more cards may meet the criteria of both categories and ask them to place such cards on the vertical line separating the two categories. Placing these cards correctly earns a 3-point bonus.
- Prepare items for the game on regular index cards, strips of paper, or self-stick paper. Doing the extra work of laminating or covering the cards with contact paper now could save you a great deal of preparation time in the months to come.
- Have teams roll their own tape. Nonplaying team members can roll the strips of tape provided and then hand a tape loop to the current player. This will speed up play and create a greater sense of team effort.
- Use a noisemaker to indicate the end of the playing round. This will add to the excitement of the game.

CUSTOMIZING DILEMMA

Size of Group

- For one player: Prepare desk versions of the game sheets. Desk versions can be played with a set of cards or an accompanying sheet listing the items to be sorted.
    - Time driven: Have one player place or write as many items as possible in the correct category before time runs out.
    - Quantity driven: Have the player match or better a standard score within a stated or an open time period.
- For larger groups:
    - Conduct several games simultaneously. Review the results of the game with the entire class.
    - Split the class into sections. Have one section play a set of games while the other section watches. Review the results of the game with the entire class.

Time of Play
- Expand or contract the time in each round depending on the difficulty or number of the items to be sorted and the level of the students.

Focus of the Task
- Allow teams to coach their players as they are placing their cards. This helps the player and keeps the rest of the team involved in each decision.

- Allow more than one player to touch a card. Teams can appoint one player as the *runner,* the person who places the card on the game sheet.

- Expand the game sheet format to represent up to four category headings.

- Place a series of math problems on index cards and have the players sort them into the two categories: Correct and Incorrect.

- Create a chart on which the categories are two or three centuries. Have players place inventions, events, or famous people in the appropriate century.

- Translate this game into a take-home or learning center exercise, as described earlier.

Scoring
- Award 5 bonus points if a team places all of its cards on the game sheet before the time expires.

- Subtract 1 point for each incorrectly placed card. This scoring dynamic affects the level of competition.

- Award 3 points for each correctly placed card, subtract 1 point for each incorrectly placed card, and give 0 points for cards not played.

- To encourage teams to place all their cards, subtract 1 point for each item not placed on the game sheet.

Dilemma

Directions Sort these numbers into the appropriate category.

3

7

8

9

10

11

12

14

21

32

41

Odd	Even

Dilemma

Team	Round 1	Round 2	Round 3
1			
2			
3			
4			
5			
Total Points			

Dilemma

- Form two to five teams.

- When instructed, the first player turns over the first card.

- The first player places the card in the appropriate column on the game sheet.

- When the first player has completed this step, the second player turns over the next card.

- Play continues until the teacher calls time.

- Scoring is as follows:

    A *correctly* placed card = 1 point

    An *incorrectly* placed card = 0 points

    A card *not played* = 0 points

- The team with the most points wins.

Fast Track

INTRODUCTION   Fast Track establishes an environment that suggests a game show. In this environment that students enjoy, you can use questions to elicit a series of related answers, taking students through a brief case study of a topic. Each team is assigned one *track* on the wall game sheet. A correct response to a question advances a team's icon up the track. The team whose icon advances the farthest wins.

This game, originally created as an ethics wall game by Steve Sugar and Carol Willett, has been reformatted for this audience.

Purpose	• To review a topic in some depth and over time.
	• To work in teams where everyone's contribution is needed to succeed.

Game Objective	To be the first team to reach "Finish."

Players	3 or more. *Can be adapted for one-on-one tutoring.*

Time	25–50 minutes.

Grades	3–8.

Supplies	• A set of 15 or more questions about the topic, developed by the teacher.
	• 1 game sheet drawn on the chalkboard or presented on the overhead.
	• 1 answer sheet for each team.

GAME STEPS

Preliminaries	• Prepare the wall game sheet in one of these ways:
	• Draw the game sheet shown at the end of this game on the chalkboard; indicate advances by filling in track spaces with chalk.
	• Draw the game sheet on a sheet of newsprint; indicate advances with movable icons made of paper or index cards *or* by filling in track spaces with a felt-tipped marker.
	• Reproduce the game sheet on an overhead transparency; indicate advances with markers, such as coins or paper clips.

- Prepare a set of answer sheets, one for each team. (See the sample at the end of this game.)

- Divide the class into two or three teams.

- Have each team select a track (1, 2, or 3) on the game sheet.

- Distribute one answer sheet to each team.

Round 1

- Present the first question.

- Have each team record its response on its answer sheet.

- Have each team present its response to the rest of the class.

- Present the correct response.

Scoring

For a *correct* response, advance the team's icon as many spaces on the game sheet as indicated by the value of the question.

For an *incorrect* response, do not move team's icon.

Round 2 to End of Game

Game is played the same way for all rounds.

End of Game

The first team to cross into the "Finish" area wins. (If no team has finished, the team closest to "Finish" is declared the winner.)

SCORING EXAMPLE

Preliminaries
- The teacher divides the class into three teams.
- Each team selects a track on the game sheet:
  - Team A selects Track 1.
  - Team B selects Track 2.
  - Team C selects Track 3.
- The teacher hands out one answer sheet to each team.

Round 1
- The teacher presents the first question, valued at 1 point.
- Each team writes down and then presents its response.
- The teacher presents the correct response.
- Teams A and C had the correct response.
- Team B had an incorrect response.
- The teacher advances the icons for Team A and C one space.
- The teacher leaves Team B's icon in "Start."

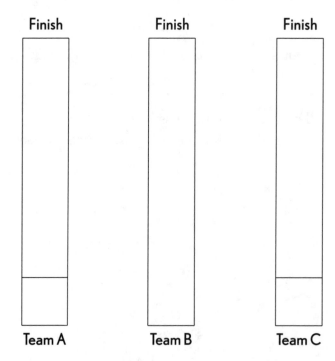

- This ends play for Round 1.

Round 2

- The teacher presents the second question, valued at 2 points.

- Each team writes down and then presents its response.

- The teacher presents the correct response.

- Teams B and C had the correct response.

- Team A had an incorrect response.

- The teacher advances the icons for Team B and C two spaces.

- The teacher leaves Team A's icon on the first space.

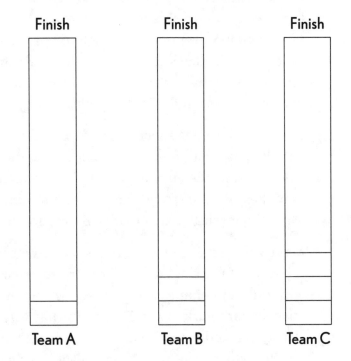

- This ends play for Round 2.

TEACHER NOTES

- This is an excellent, visual way to review a topic with the entire class. The game sheet creates the atmosphere of a race. The teacher can add to that environment by varying the type of questions (by topic and by format) and by changing each question's value (awarding 1, 2, or 3 points). This will allow teams who seem to be way back to have a chance on the very next turn.

- This game allows you to introduce more challenging question formats, such as a mini-case study requiring a series of three or four responses. In this way you can acquaint your students with more complex group problem-solving processes and give them immediate feedback on their decisions. Repeated use of case studies can help students gain an understanding of the decision-making process and critical thinking.

- Re-create the game sheet on the floor of the gym or playground, and then use this game as a physical activity. Ask student volunteers to act as the marking icons. When a team responds to a question, these walking icons move the appropriate number of spaces. This will physically involve all children in the play of the game.

- Make an overhead of the game sheet, and conduct the game from the front of the class. You may want to use a variety of objects with different shapes as icons, such as a penny, paper clip, chalk stick, square magnet, and so on. In that way, each team can clearly see and identify with its shape and will even remind the teacher which icon to advance on the overhead chart.

- The requirement that teams write down their response for each question should eliminate disputes over whether a team has "copied" another team's response during the reporting (team presentation) sessions. If this question is nevertheless raised, that may be a good time to cover issues of fairness, honesty, and interteam cooperation.

- This game encourages teams to seek input from everyone in the group. This behavior can be reinforced during closure when the teacher asks each team how it came up with its ideas. Inevitably, teams with the most progress up the track will reveal that they asked all players for input.

- Use this game as a continuing weeklong event related to one topic or one curriculum segment. Keep the game sheet visible all week, and play one or two rounds the first thing every morning. Such extended use of the game can focus on application of the topic and reinforce take-home study.

- Use this game as an open-book test during which the teams can look up information in their notes or any other reference material. As long as the team meets the time deadlines for answers, any form of seeking and learning goes. This familiarizes students with the intensity of test taking without their having to work in isolation or respond to questions without reference material. It also reinforces class readings and notes.

CUSTOMIZING FAST TRACK

Size of Group

- For one player: Play the game with the student standing up at a wall chart or sitting down at a table game sheet.

  - Time driven: Have the player respond to a series of questions in her attempt to move as many spaces as she can up the track before time runs out.

  - Quantity driven: See how many spaces the player can move up the track over a standard number of questions.

- For small groups: Divide the students into two teams.

- For medium-size groups: Divide the students into five teams of three to five players per team. Create a larger game sheet using five tracks. Be sure to allow for more time to discuss and evaluate the listed items and be sure to review the results of the game with the entire class.

- For large groups: Divide the students into two sections of five teams each. Have one section play a set of games while the other section watches. Review the results of the game with the entire class.

Time of Play

- Shorten or lengthen the time for a round of play, depending on the difficulty of the question material or the class's level of understanding.

- Expand or contract the number of rounds of play.

- Conduct as a weeklong game.

Focus of the Task

- Assign a teacher's assistant, or *coach,* to each team to guide it in the decision-making process.

- Create several sets of questions on different topics. Allow the teams to select the next topic.

- Assign one or more case studies as a take-home exercise, and in the next class, conduct the game using as a topic all or some of the assigned case studies.

Scoring

- Assign different values to different question formats and then allow one of the teams (preferably the lowest-scoring team up to that point) to select the next question format. Suggested question format values: True-false = 1 point, multiple choice = 2 points, direct question = 3 points, case study = 5 points.

- Create a set of *risk* questions for which the icon moves *up* a specified number of spaces for a correct response and *down* a space for an incorrect response.

Fast Track

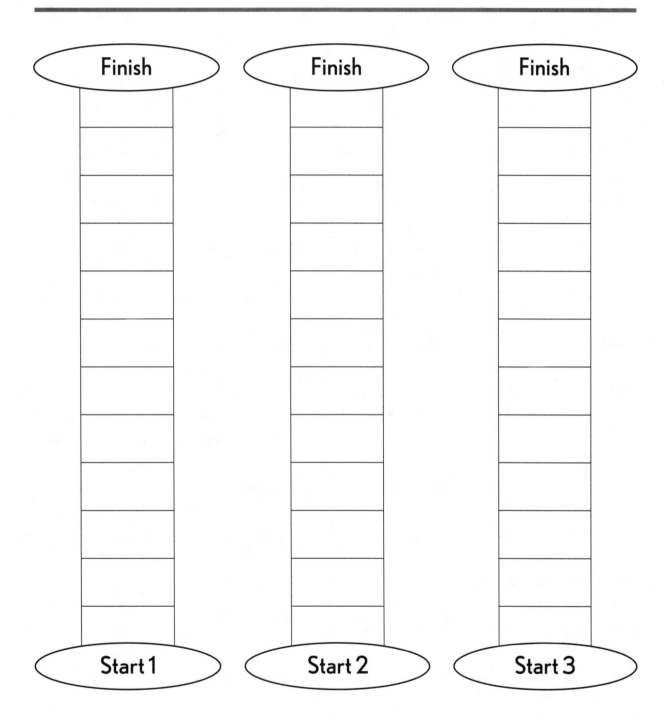

Fast Track

Team Name _____

Question 1. _____

Question 2. _____

Question 3. _____

Question 4. _____

Question 5. _____

Question 6. _____

Question 7. _____

Question 8. _____

Question 9. _____

Question 10. _____

Question 11. _____

Question 12. _____

Question 13. _____

Question 14. _____

- Form two or three teams.

- The teacher presents the first question.

- Write your response on the answer sheet. Tell the teacher your response when he or she asks for it.

- Scoring is as follows:

   For a *correct* response, your team's icon advances up the track.

   For an *incorrect* response, your team's icon remains in place.

- The first team to reach "Finish" wins.

GRAB BAG

INTRODUCTION   Because Grab Bag gives students special rewards for correct answers, it is best used as a special day game, for celebrations or closures. Teams write out answers to a series of curriculum topic questions. When one or more of the teams receives 11 points, each winning team member earns a trip to the grab bag to pull for a surprise. Once the grab bag concept has been established, many variations can be used.

| **Purpose** | • To engage in active problem solving and team decision making. |
| | • To objectively reward knowledge of a topic. |

Game Objective To collect enough points to earn one or more trips to the grab bag.

Players 4 or more. *Can be adapted for one-on-one tutoring.*

Time 15–45 minutes.

Grades K–8.

Supplies	• 1 set of questions, prepared in advance by the teacher.
	• 1 response sheet for each team.
	• 1 small paper bag, the *grab bag*.
	• Several slips of paper identifying varying prizes.
	• The prizes themselves (if they are tangible objects).
	• Paper and pencils for each team.

GAME STEPS

| **Preliminaries** | • Divide the class into two to five teams. |
| | • Distribute one response sheet to each team. |

Round 1	• Present the first question.
	• Have each team record its response on its response sheet.
	• Call time; have each team present its response to the rest of the class.
	• Present the correct response.

Scoring	A *correct* response = 1 point

A *correct* response = 1 point

An *incorrect* response = 0 points

Record each team's score on the chalkboard.

Round 2 to End of Game

All rounds are played in a similar fashion.

End of Game

When one or more teams receives 11 points, each member of the winning team or teams earns a trip to the grab bag.

SCORING EXAMPLE

Preliminaries

- The class is divided into three teams: Team A, Team B, and Team C.

- The teacher hands out one response sheet to each team.

Round 1

- The teacher presents the first question.

- Each team writes down its response on the response sheet.

- The teacher calls time.

- Each team presents its response to the rest of the class.

- The teacher goes over the question and the correct response.

- Team A and Team C had correct responses.

- The teacher awards 1 point to Team A and 1 point to Team C.

- The teacher posts the team scores on the chalkboard:

	Team A	Team B	Team C
Round 1	1	–	1

- This ends play for Round 1.

Round 2

- The teacher presents the second question.

- Teams B and C had correct responses.

- The teacher awards 1 point to Team B and 1 point to Team C.

	Team A	Team B	Team C
Round 1	1	–	1
Round 2	–	1	1

- This ends play for Round 2.

Round 3 to End of Game

- Play continues in this fashion until Team B earns 11 points.

- The teacher announces:

  "Team B—go to the grab bag."

- The teacher then has each member of Team B come up front and reach into the grab bag and pull out a prize slip.

TEACHER NOTES

- Getting rewards is not an everyday activity but a treat. This is a special game for special days—days when your class was extra productive, the day before a long vacation, or days on which you want to bring the week to a fun closure.

- Used in home schooling, this game can commemorate a special date, such as the child's birthday, linking academics to that date in a special way.

- Requiring teams to write down their responses should eliminate any questions about whether a team has "copied" another team's response during the reporting (team presentation) phase of the game. But if such questions are raised, that may be a good time to cover issues of fairness, honesty, and interteam cooperation.

- Each teacher has her own philosophy on motivating children and on whether rewards, tangible or otherwise, are appropriate. If you feel uncomfortable with using tangible rewards for classroom achievement, then you might pass on this game.

- Eleven points is our recommended goal because it is high enough to challenge players to keep their eye on the prize. Offering prizes for fewer points, such as 5 or 7, may result in frequent trips to the grab bag, which will slow down play.

- Vary the game so that everyone wins. Have a runners-up grab bag, or play until everyone reaches 11 points. Let the winning team pass out prizes to teams that came in second and third.

- After the first team reaches 11 points, introduce *bonus* questions. When the other teams respond correctly to these questions, they too earn a trip to the grab bag.

- Create "gold," "silver," and "bronze" bags. Have each team play until it achieves 11 points, but the first team to reach the goal goes to the gold bag, the second team goes to the silver bag, and the third team goes to the bronze bag. Emphasize that each team has won; it just took some teams less time than others, just as in the Olympics.

- Allow any team member to pass on reaching into the bag. The player may not want to come to the front of the room or may not want to take the risk of not getting the prize he wants. Whatever the reason, you can use this event to start a discussion of risk and even of refusal skills.

- You are the best judge of what is *special* for your class. Consider these prize ideas:

  - Stickers

  - Special pencils

  - Eraser heads

  - "Get out of homework" cards

  - "Extra recess" cards

  - "First selection" cards for library or treat tables

  - Key rings

  - Name tags with "Special Merit" written on them

  - Magnets

  - Gum (with the rule that it is to be chewed outside of the classroom)

  - "First in line" cards, for recess or going home

  - Baseball cards

  - Team riddles that when solved lead to a *treasure* hidden in the room

- Consider these techniques for prize management:

  - If you do not want students to trade prizes, write each child's name on the back of the prize slip she draws. This will ensure that you know who should get that prize.

  - If you have a set of Bobbsey twins, two children who are inseparable, and only one of them receives the prize of an extra recess, it might be a problem. To avoid this situation, you might allow students to trade prizes that are similar.

  - If you plan to have an extra recess as a prize, you may have to arrange for a teaching assistant or parent volunteer.

  - Make sure that prizes offering special privileges are cashed in as soon as possible. Children quickly return to normal routines. When a child invokes a special privilege earned one week ago, it will be a cause for disruption.

- Add to the game environment by using a noisemaker to announce when a team has earned a trip to the grab bag.

- For younger students: Walk to each table during play to make sure students understand the rules and to review their responses before they present them to the rest of the class. This *walking tour* can be eliminated if you feel that the teams understand the game and are playing fairly.

- For older students: Use the grab bag to dispense *activity* slips as well as prizes. These slips can award bonus points, penalty points, or an extra turn at the grab bag or might require the team to perform an activity such as singing "Happy Birthday" to the rest of the class or reciting a poem.

- Once the students associate the grab bag with fun surprises, use the bag to exchange or trade objects, contain questions, or suggest events. For example:

  - Use the bag as an *activity* bag. Create activities or have your students write out their activity requests, and then have a student draw one activity from the bag, such as selecting a song for a sing-along.

  - Use the bag as the holder of mystery letters, numbers, words, pictures, or questions for the class to identify or answer.

  - Use the bag as part of a Truth or Consequences game. If a team answers a question correctly, it gets points. If it misses a question, it draws a consequence from the bag, such as having to laugh aloud for fifteen seconds or some other fun consequence.

  - Use the bag as a miscellaneous *task* bag, allowing students to choose between an assigned task or a task randomly drawn from the task bag.

  - Use the bag as a *give-and-take* bag. Each student puts in a small token or prize, and these prizes are drawn as rewards or for successfully accomplishing a classroom assignment.

CUSTOMIZING GRAB BAG

Size of Group

- For one player:

  - Time driven: Challenge the player to answer a series of questions correctly, responding to seven questions within a stated time. If he beats the clock, then he gets a turn at the grab bag.

  - Quantity driven: Give the player a series of short tests, using from five to seven questions per test. The player earns 1 point for missing only one response or missing no responses and a bonus of 1 point (for a total of 2 points) for answering all seven questions correctly. Award the player a chance at the grab bag when he reaches 11 points.

- For larger groups: Award *team* prizes, such as special privileges, the next class day.

Time of Play

- Shorten the game by lowering the points required to win to 5 or 7. Lengthen the game by raising the points required to 21.

Focus of the Task

- Have each team keep its own response sheet at its table and give its responses orally.

- Present a problem statement. Have each team present its solution. Award points for best solution, best presentation, and so forth.

- Present a set of five to seven problems or questions. If a team answers all but one correctly, it gets 1 point. If a team answers all correctly, it also gets a bonus point for a total of 2 points.

- Present a problem statement to be solved within a set time. Award bonus points for being the first team to solve the statement and for the most correct solution.

- Use a second grab bag as a generator of randomly ordered questions. Have one of the players reach into this *question* bag and then read a question for the next round of play.

Scoring

- For older students: Change the scoring system to "the most points" wins a trip to the grab bag.

Grab Bag

Team Name _____

Question 1. _____ Points _____

Question 2. _____ Points _____

Question 3. _____ Points _____

Question 4. _____ Points _____

Question 5. _____ Points _____

Question 6. _____ Points _____

Question 7. _____ Points _____

Question 8. _____ Points _____

Question 9. _____ Points _____

Question 10. _____ Points _____

Question 11. _____ Points _____

Question 12. _____ Points _____

Question 13. _____ Points _____

Question 14. _____ Points _____

Question 15. _____ Points _____

Question 16. _____ Points _____

Grab Bag

- Form two or more teams.

- The teacher presents the first question.

- Write your response on your response sheet.

- Present your response to the rest of the class.

  Each *correct* response = 1 point

- When a team earns 11 points, each team member gets a trip to the grab bag.

GRANNY SQUARES

INTRODUCTION Granny Squares is an in-chair game that everyone can easily take part in, and it offers students a chance to outguess their teacher. Before asking a question, the teacher covers one square of a four-square grid on her master game sheet, and players on each team mark the square they deduce she has covered. When the teacher offers hints, this process involves some imaginative problem solving as well as guessing. The teacher then asks a question. The score for each round is a combination of the correctness of the response and the correctness of the square selection.

| **Purpose** | • To improve understanding of the topic. |
| | • To apply problem-solving skills in situations where there is a high degree of uncertainty. |

| **Game Objective** | To score the most points. |

| **Players** | 4 or more. *Can be adapted for one-on-one tutoring.* |

| **Time** | 15–45 minutes. |

| **Grades** | K–8. |

Supplies	• A set of questions, prepared in advance by the teacher.
	• 1 marker (a chip or other small object) for the teacher to use.
	• 1 game sheet per player or team of players.
	• 1 master game sheet for the teacher.
	• Paper and pencils for the players.

GAME STEPS

Preliminaries	• Divide the class into teams of two to four players.
	• Distribute one game sheet to each player or team of players.
	• Set up the teacher's master game sheet.

| **Round 1** | • Without revealing the space chosen, place your marker on one of the four squares of the grid on line 1 of the game sheet. |
| | • Optional: Give a clue about the location of the marker. |

- Have each team select and then mark the square they think you covered.

- Present the first question.

- Have each team write down its response. (Younger players may give an answer orally to a team *observer*.)

- Go over the correct response, and have players self-score.

Question Scoring

A *correct* response = 3 points

An *incorrect* response = 0 points

Square Selection Scoring (Bonus Point)

Correct selection of the covered square = 1 point

Incorrect selection of the covered square = 0 points

Teams enter their points on their game sheets.

Round 2 to End of Game

All rounds are played in the same fashion.

End of Game

Teams total their points, and the team with the most points wins.

SCORING EXAMPLE

Preliminaries

- The fifth-grade class is divided into three teams: A, B, and C.

- Each team receives a game sheet.

Round 1

- The teacher covers the upper-left square of the grid on line 1.

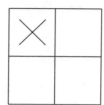

- The teacher gives the clue "north by northwest."

- The teacher instructs each team to mark, on line 1 of its game sheet, the square the players think the teacher covered.

Team A   Team B   Team C

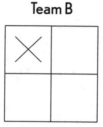   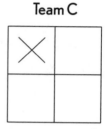

- The teacher presents the question, and each team writes its response on line 1 of the game sheet.

- The teacher calls time.

- Each team presents its response to the rest of the class.

Scoring

Team A:	Gave a *correct* response	= 3 points
	Did *not* select the covered square	= 0 points
	Total	= 3 points
Team B:	Gave an *incorrect* response	= 0 points
	Selected the covered square	= 1 point
	Total	= 1 point
Team C:	Gave a *correct* response	= 3 points
	Selected the covered square	= 1 point
	Total	= 4 points

TEACHER NOTES

- This is an excellent way to involve even the most reluctant student. Because the play revolves around two factors—guessing the covered square and then responding to the question—no one is ever left out of the game process.

- In a sense the challenge of selecting the covered square drives the learning. This game encourages students to participate through the fascination of trying to outguess the teacher.

- Use this game to promote skills in "patterning," guessing the position of the next square to be covered given previous placements.

- Use this game following highly active periods, such as recess, or after a long holiday.

- Use this game to add variety to subject recall in tutoring sessions with two or three students.

- Allow teams to rotate the *guessing* role among the players to see which one seems best at anticipating the teacher. This will also encourage greater involvement.

- Because teams self-score on their game sheets, the issue of cheating may arise. Use this situation to start a discussion of ethics—fairness versus winning at any cost.

- Vary the response time allowed by grade level and topic. By announcing the time allotted before play begins, you will be training students in how to manage their time as they would on standardized tests.

- For younger groups: Use the Granny Squares grid to reinforce topic information:

  - Use the grid to reinforce concepts of *position* (up and down, left and right, top and bottom), and then use these concepts when giving hints about the covered square.

  - Use various colors on the grid squares to reinforce color identification, and then give hints about the color of the covered square.

- Number the squares to reinforce specific numbers or Roman numerals, and then give numeric hints or hold up fingers to help students find the covered square.

- Letter the squares to reinforce specific letters, and then give hints about the starting letter of a familiar animal, vegetable, or mineral to help students find the covered square.

- This game can be used to introduce new material in math language skills. Simply place a number or letter in each of the Granny Square boxes, then give a hint, such as describing a math problem that has a solution in one of the boxes or holding up an object that starts with a letter placed in a box. Because the solutions are part of the bonus, the new information can be considered as part of the game.

- First-time users may find it helpful to complete the entire gamesheet—clues and all—before they play. This will allow them to focus on providing the correct answers and guiding their students in scoring.

CUSTOMIZING GRANNY SQUARES

Size of Group

- For one player: Use this game as a one-on-one activity pitting the student's "intuition" against the covered square selections of the teacher. Give hints about the location of the square as needed, to encourage greater student involvement and success.

- For small and medium-size groups: Have sets of two teams play against each other. Have one team cover a square. If the opposing team correctly selects the covered square, *both* teams receive a bonus of 2 points. This is a good way to encourage a win-win philosophy. If you feel that teams are collaborating unfairly, you may want to invoke a discussion about "fair play."

- For large groups:

  - Conduct several games simultaneously. Review the results of the game with the entire class.

  - Split the class into sections. Have one section play a set of games while the other section watches. Review the results of the game with the entire class.

Time of Play

- Set time limits within which teams must answer questions.

- Play for a specific length of time or number of rounds.

Focus of the Task

- For each round, select one team to cover the square, and have all other teams try to guess the covered square. Award points to both the team that selects the correct square and the team(s) that covered it. Observe any efforts to collaborate or collude on the part of the team selected to cover the space. If collusion occurs, invoke a discussion on "fair play."

- For younger groups: Identify the squares with colors, numbers, or letters to reinforce identification skills, and then give clues to help the teams identify the covered square, as described earlier.

Scoring

- For younger groups: Increase the bonus for guessing the covered square.

- For older groups: Increase the points received for a correct response to the question.

Granny Squares

Question 1. _____ Points _____

Question 2. _____ Points _____

Question 3. _____ Points _____

Question 4. _____ Points _____

Question 5. _____ Points _____

Question 6. _____ Points _____

Question 7. _____ Points _____

Question 8. _____ Points _____

Question 9. _____ Points _____

Question 10. _____ Points _____

Granny Squares

- Form into teams.

- The teacher secretly covers one of the granny squares.

- On line 1 of your game sheet, mark the square you think the teacher covered.

- Respond to the first question.

- Score your game sheet as follows:

  A *correct* response = 3 points

  An *incorrect* response = 0 points

  Correct selection of the covered square = 1 point

  Incorrect selection of the covered square = 0 points

- After all the questions are answered, the team with the most points wins.

GUESSTIMATE

INTRODUCTION

Guesstimate can familiarize students with the standardized test-taking task of answering sets of questions in a specific format in a limited time. Moreover, it allows students the safety of working on this process in teams. Before answering a series of questions, each team estimates the number it will answer correctly. Team scores are based largely on the accuracy of this estimate and are intended to reward a certain level of risk taking. The game can be played as often as necessary to cover the material.

This game, originally created as a testing game for *Games That Teach,* by Steve Sugar, has been reformatted for this audience.

Purpose	• To increase understanding of definitions and concepts from the readings and lesson material.
	• To practice using different testing formats.
	• To experience the rewards and consequences of risk taking.

Game Objective	To win by scoring the most team points.

Players	6 or more. *Can be adapted for one-on-one tutoring.*

Time	25–45 minutes.

Grades	4–8.

Supplies	• 1 set of question sheets for each team, per round.
	• Paper and pencils for each team.

GAME STEPS

Preliminaries	Divide class into two or more teams of three to five players each.

Round 1	• Inform teams they will be given five minutes to answer a set of seven questions.
	• Have each team estimate how many correct responses it will provide.
	• Post each team's estimate on the chalkboard.
	• Distribute one copy of question sheet 1 for each player.
	• After five minutes, collect one completed question sheet from each team.

- Review the answers, and tally each team's number of actual correct responses.

- Using the numbers for each team's estimated and actual correct responses, compute the scores using the Point Finder Grid.

- Record each team's points on the chalkboard.

Round 2 to End of Game

Each round is played in the same fashion.

End of Game
- Total all team points.

- The team with the most points wins.

SCORING EXAMPLE

Preliminaries

The class is divided into three teams: Team A, Team B, and Team C.

Round 1
- The teacher asks each team to predict how many correct responses it will get on a set of seven questions. The students have *not* seen the questions at this point. The teacher advises them that the questions are about the take-home readings.

- The teacher records their *estimates* of their correct responses:

	Team A	Team B	Team C
Estimated	6	5	4

- Each team receives one set of question sheet 1, one sheet per player.

- The teacher informs the teams that they have five minutes and begins play.

- Time is called after five minutes.

- The teacher collects one completed question sheet from each team.

- The teacher goes over the correct responses to the seven questions with the class.

- The teacher tallies the *actual correct responses,* as follows:

Round 1	Team A	Team B	Team C
Estimated	6	5	4
Actual	5	6	6

- The teacher locates the team scores on the Point Finder Grid.

  Team A: Estimated = 6   Actual = 5   Points = 10

  Team B: Estimated = 5   Actual = 6   Points = 27

  Team C: Estimated = 4   Actual = 6   Points = 20

- Team scores at the end of Round 1:

Team A	Team B	Team C
10	27	20

Round 2

- The teacher asks each team to predict how many correct responses it will get on a second set of seven questions. She advises the players that the questions are about the last lesson in their mathematics curriculum.

- Each team estimates its number of correct responses to the second set of seven questions.

- The teacher records their *estimates* of their correct responses:

	Team A	Team B	Team C
Estimated	5	7	6

- The teacher distributes one copy of question sheet 2 to each player on each team.

- The teams are given five minutes to respond to question sheet 2.

- After calling time, the teacher collects the question sheets and reviews the correct responses.

- The teacher tallies the *actual correct responses,* as follows:

Round 2	Team A	Team B	Team C
Estimated	5	7	6
Actual	5	6	6

- The teacher locates the team scores on the Point Finder Grid.

    Team A: Estimated = 5   Actual = 5   Points = 25

    Team B: Estimated = 7   Actual = 6   Points = 12

    Team C: Estimated = 6   Actual = 6   Points = 36

- Team scores at the end of Round 2:

	Team A	Team B	Team C
Round 1	10	27	20
Round 2	25	12	36
Total	35	39	56

Round 3: Final Round

- The teacher asks each team to predict how many correct responses it will get on a set of seven questions. She advises the players that the questions are about their latest assignment in social studies.

- Each team estimates its number of correct responses.

- The teacher records their *estimates* of their correct responses:

	Team A	Team B	Team C
Estimated	6	6	6

- The teams are given five minutes to respond to question sheet 3.

- After calling time, the teacher collects the question sheets and reviews the correct responses.

- The teacher tallies the *actual correct responses,* as follows:

Round 3	Team A	Team B	Team C
Estimated	6	6	6
Actual	7	6	5

- The teacher locates the team scores on the Point Finder Grid.

  Team A: Estimated = 6   Actual = 7   Points = 38

  Team B: Estimated = 6   Actual = 6   Points = 36

  Team C: Estimated = 6   Actual = 5   Points = 10

- Team scores at the end of Round 3:

	Team A	Team B	Team C
Round 1	10	27	20
Round 2	25	12	36
Round 3	38	36	10
Total	73	75	66

End of Game   The teacher announces that Team B, with 75 points, is the winner.

TEACHER NOTES

- With the increased emphasis on standardized testing, this is one of the best ways to get students used to responding to sets of questions in a short time. You can create questions that review your material in the formats commonly used on standardized tests. This will help students mentally prepare for any test as they enjoy playing a competitive game.

- This game can reduce test anxiety among both students and teachers. The students will become more accustomed to various testing formats, yet do so free from the burden of such anxiety.

- This has proven to be a powerful game for reinforcing previous lessons or take-home assignments. Students become much more diligent in their efforts because they do not want to embarrass themselves in front of classmates.

- Reviewing the question sets at the end of each round gives you an excellent opportunity to reinforce the material by underscoring the reasons the selected answer is the best answer.

- When students take issue with a correct response, remember that this means they are actively involved in the topic and are now open to learning the *why* and not just the *what* of the question.

- Reinforce learning about the test-taking process by going over tips on taking written examinations as you go over the correct answers.

- Ask your students if they have tips on how to respond correctly to test questions. This can lead to a discussion on ways to deal with written questions—a mini-lesson in how to take a test.

- Small groups and this game's format allow each team to have an in-depth discussion on the set of questions. Going over the questions in this way provides elaboration and additional reinforcement of the topic.

- Creating a nonthreatening environment by using small groups encourages even the most timid student to participate.

- Group students into random teams, teaming them with class-mates who may not be in their peer group. This is a wonderful opportunity for students to get to know and work with each other.

- For older student teams: Allow them to grade their own papers. This can open a discussion on issues of empowerment and ethics.

- Understanding the scoring system:

  - The Point Finder Grid instantly tells you how many points to award each team. The grid also serves as a visual reminder that higher risk taking can lead to higher scores. Make an overhead transparency of the grid to reinforce this concept during game play.

  - The scoring system is *contract* scoring. When a team makes its estimate, it is establishing a numerical contract. The payoff is the number of correct responses squared. Thus, if a team achieves its contract, it receives the square of its original estimate. *All* additional correct responses are awarded 2 points each.

    Example 1: A team estimates it will make five correct responses but actually makes six. It receives 25 points (for meeting its contract) plus 2 points (for the additional correct response) for a total of 27 points.

    Example 2: A team estimates it will make two correct responses but actually makes six. It receives only 4 points (for meeting its contract) plus 8 points (2 points for each additional correct response) for a total of 12 points. (Thus, the team that took the greater risk of contracting for six correct responses received an additional 24 points for its effort, whereas the team that hedged its estimate received only 12 points altogether for an almost perfect test score.)

    Example 3: A team estimates it will make six correct responses, but makes only five. This team did *not* meet its contract, so each correct response receives 2 points, for a total of 10 points.

- Why give 2 points for correct responses that go beyond the contracted number? Simply, we believe that you should reward achievement, even if the reward is not at the top level.

CUSTOMIZING GUESSTIMATE

Size of Group

- For one player: Have the player attempt to collect as many points as she can over three or more rounds. Use past scores as *par* for future game play.

- For two players:

  - Have the two students play together as a team, working to collect as many points as they can over three or more rounds.

  - Have the two students play against each other. This can be a dynamic way to reinforce material.

Time of Play

- Shorten or lengthen the time allowed for the responses to correspond with the difficulty of the topic, the complexity of the questions, and the players' ability. Thus you might allow an older group only three or four minutes to answer a set of seven questions, but a younger group might be allowed ten minutes.

- Vary the number of rounds in accordance with the available time.

Focus of the Task

- Vary the question formats. This will also prepare the students for the varied formats of the questions used in standardized testing.

- Consider using this game as an introduction to new material. When working in teams and within the game format, players will focus on the topic and not feel threatened.

- After collecting the question sheets but before reviewing the correct responses, allow each team to revise its estimate of its correct responses. This *reality check* is often an excellent chance for students to vent—removing some of the anxiety associated with making estimates before answering the questions. For scoring purposes, you may (1) hold each team accountable for its *original* estimate (a strategy that may lead to discussions of responsibility and accountability) *or* (2) accept the revisions as the *working* estimate, removing some of the students' test anxiety.

- For older students:

  - Allow them to keep the question sheets and their notes as a review set of structured notes on the topic.

  - Allow them to use books or other desk references in an open-book setting. This can underscore the value of homework and other outside readings.

Scoring

- Allow extra points for questions of extra complexity or importance.

- Use sets of four, five, or six questions, using the same scoring system of squaring the original estimate, with additional correct responses earning 2 points.

- Be prepared with a *tie-breaker* question—a difficult, but vital question—to use in the event two or more teams tie for first place.

POINT FINDER GRID
Guesstimate

How to find the number of points earned by each team:

1. Locate the number of estimated correct responses in the left column.

2. Track across the top row to the number of actual correct responses.

3. Read the points in the square where the selected row and selected column intersect.

(For example, if the estimated number = 5 and the actual number = 6, then the points earned = 27.)

Estimated Number of Correct Responses	Actual Number of Correct Responses						
	1	2	3	4	5	6	7
1	1	3	5	7	9	11	13
2	2	4	6	8	10	12	14
3	2	4	9	11	13	15	17
4	2	4	6	16	18	20	22
5	2	4	6	8	25	27	29
6	2	4	6	8	10	36	38
7	2	4	6	8	10	12	49

Guesstimate

Round	Team	Team	Team	Team	Team
1					
2					
3					
4					
5					
Total Points					

Guesstimate

- Form teams of three to five players.

- Estimate the number of questions your team feels it will answer correctly.

- You have five minutes to respond to each question sheet.

- The teacher tallies your actual number of correct responses and computes the appropriate number of points.

- The game is played the same way for all rounds.

- The team with the most points wins.

GUGGENHEIM

INTRODUCTION   Guggenheim makes a good take-home assignment but is also a good game for teams because it is easy for everyone to participate. This game rewards originality and encourages students to think more broadly. In the classroom the game is played on a wall chart that shows a matrix, or grid, with letters on the horizontal axis and categories on the vertical axis. Each team writes down as many items as it can think of for each category combined with each letter. Each team then receives 1 point for each item and a 5-point bonus for placing at least one item in each game sheet square.

This game, originally created as a brainstorming exercise for *Games That Teach Teams,* by Steve Sugar and George Takacs, has been reformatted for this audience.

Purpose	• To promote the ability to brainstorm and think imaginatively.
	• To reinforce identification of letters in relation to topic items.

Game Objective	To score the most points.

Players	6 or more. *Can be adapted for one-on-one tutoring.*

Time	15–40 minutes.

Grades	3–8.

Supplies	• 1 wall game sheet for each team.
	• Felt-tipped markers or crayons.
	• Masking tape, to post large game sheets on the wall.

GAME STEPS

Preliminaries	Divide the class into teams of three to five players each.

Round 1	• Give each team a wall game sheet.
	• Give teams seven minutes to think of and write down as many items as they can that are suggested by the forced association of each letter with each category on the game sheet.
	• Call time at the end of seven minutes.

Scoring	Each *correctly* identified item = 1 point
	Placing at least one item in each square = 5 points

Round 2 to End of Game

All rounds are played the same way.

End of Game

The team with the most points wins.

SCORING EXAMPLE

Preliminaries

- The teacher prepares one flip chart–sized game sheet per team, as follows (see the sample game and the sample game sheet on page 240):

- The teacher draws a two-by-three matrix.

- On the vertical (y) axis, he lists two categories: "Something to Eat" and "Something to Wear."

- On the horizontal (x) axis, he places three letters: "A," "B," and "C."

- The class is divided into two teams.

- Each team meets at a game sheet taped to the wall or placed on a table. Each team has crayons or felt-tipped markers available.

Round 1

The teacher starts the game and calls time after seven minutes of play.

Scoring

- Team A's game sheet contains these items:

  - Something to eat: (A) *apple, applesauce, apple pie;* (B) *banana, bagel, bread, blue cheese;* (C) *corn, crab, cake, cream, cheese, coffee, candy.*

  - Something to wear: (B) *bathing suit, boxer shorts, baseball hat, boots;* (C) *cap, coat.*

- The teacher awards the following points:

  14 items for "Eat" = 14 points

  6 items for "Wear" = <u>6 points</u>

  Total items listed = 20 points

  Bonus points   = <u>0 points*</u>

  Total   = 20 points

Team did not identify an "A" item under "Something to Wear."

- Team B's game sheet contains these items:

  - Something to eat: (A) *apple, apple butter;* (B) *beef, butter, butterscotch, barbecue chicken;* (C) *crab, chowder, clam chowder, clams, cereal.*

  - Something to wear: (A) *armband;* (B) *bathrobe, boots, baseball hat;* (C) *cape, cap, coat.*

- The teacher awards the following points:

  11 items for "Eat" = 11 points

  7 items for "Wear" = <u>7 points</u>

  Total items listed = 18 points

  Bonus points   = <u>5 points*</u>

  Total   = 23 points

Team identified at least one item in each square on the game sheet.

TEACHER NOTES

- This game rewards originality. Too often tests and worksheets ask merely for one correct answer, requiring everyone to come up with exactly the same response. This game encourages children to expand their way of thinking and to become originals—a priceless life skill.

- Create your own game format to elicit words specific to your students, locale, or curriculum.

- Use this game to prepare students for upcoming topic areas by issuing it as a take-home puzzle to be completed before the next class. The next day, place the students in work groups, and have these groups complete one game sheet. This group activity will give the students a more encompassing overview of the topic. Because students do not like to look foolish in front of their classmates, this exercise reinforces the importance of take-home assignments.

- This game encourages teams to seek input from everyone in the group. Reinforce this at the end of a game by asking each team how it came up with its ideas. Inevitably, the teams with the higher scores will reveal that they solicited input from all their members.

- This game demonstrates that having players of different types can ensure the needed range of input. The more extroverted players may take charge in the beginning but turn to the shyer members for their contributions as the game evolves.

- This game is different from a fill-in-the-blank test, requiring more imagination and organization. Children are collaborating with their ideas and placing the ideas into categories, giving them a new way to organize classroom information.

- For younger grades: Have children place pictures of items in the appropriate squares. This will teach them the correct association of picture and letter and category.

- Award a 3-point bonus for any item *not found* on another team's game sheet. This method takes a little longer but reinforces original thinking.

- Use a noisemaker to introduce a special or unusual item.

CUSTOMIZING GUGGENHEIM

Size of Group

- For one player: Conduct the game with the student standing up at a wall chart or sitting down at a game sheet.

  - Time driven: Have the player identify and place as many items as he can in the correct letter and category squares before the set time runs out.

  - Quantity driven: Have the player match or better a standard number of items within a stated or open time period. Allow the player to return to the same game sheet at a later time to add items.

- For small groups (four to eight players): Divide the group into two teams. Award a 3-point bonus for any item not found on the opponent's list.

- For larger groups:

  - Allow more time to discuss and evaluate the listed items.

  - Conduct several games simultaneously. Review the results of the game with the entire class.

  - Split the class into sections. Have one section play a set of games while the other section watches. Review the results of the game with the entire class.

Time of Play

- Shorten or lengthen the time for a round of play.

- Expand or contract the number of categories and letters, that is, make the game sheet matrix larger or smaller as required.

Focus of the Task

- Place numbers, centuries, or dates across the x-axis and general topic areas along the y-axis. Use this version of the game to help students develop a sense of the sequence in which important events took place.

- Use the game sheets as take-home assignments to supplement reading material or to prepare students for the next lesson.

- Keep game sheets and directions for this game in the learning center.

- Accommodate the categories in your topic and make the game more or less complex by changing the size of the matrix: two-by-two, two-by-three, three-by-three, three-by-four, and so forth.

- To involve all the students, make everyone a *recorder* by distributing crayons to all the players.

- Have each team present the items in one square of its game sheet to the rest of the class. The teacher can then survey the other teams for additional items for this square.

- For older students:

  - Rotate the game sheets among the teams for each new round of play. Continue this until all teams have played on all game sheets. This will demonstrate that creativity is a continuing event and that no matter how well one team does, others can still add to the list.

  - Have the students play *random rounds* by drawing the letters to be used from one container (such as a hat or bowl) with a number of letters written on slips of paper and then drawing the categories from another container with a number of varied categories.

Scoring

Award a three-point bonus to the team that lists an item *not found* on any opponent's game sheet.

Guggenheim

See how many items you can write in each square that are suggested by matching the letter with the category.

	A	B	C
Something to Eat	Apples Apple cider	Banana Bagels	Cheese Cream
Something to Wear	Armband Anklet	Bathing suit Baseball hat	Cardigan Clogs

Guggenheim

See how many items you can write in each square that are suggested by matching the letter with the category.

	First Letter	Second Letter	Third Letter
Category One			
Category Two			

Guggenheim

- Divide into two or more teams.

- Each team meets at a prepared game sheet.

- Develop a list of the items suggested by the combinations of categories and letters on the game sheet, and write these items in the appropriate squares.

  Each *correctly* identified item = 1 point

  Placing at least one item in each square = 5 points

- The team with the most points wins.

KNOWLEDGE GOLF

INTRODUCTION Knowledge Golf lends itself to the study of somewhat complex topics. It give students a safe environment in which to experiment with problem solving realistically, that is, from putting together clues presented one at a time. Each clue received about the identity of an item counts as taking a *stroke*. *Par* is the minimum number of clues likely to be needed to identify the item. For a less competitive environment, students can play against par rather than each other. The number of clues actually needed to identify the item determines each team's score, and as in golf, the *lowest* number of strokes wins.

| **Purpose** | • To promote critical thinking and problem solving. |
| | • To engage in interaction with the information and the other players. |

Game Objective   To score the lowest number of strokes.

Players   3 or more. *Can be adapted for one-on-one tutoring.*

Time   20–35 minutes.

Grades   3–8.

Supplies
- 4 to 9 problems, consisting of sets of clues, prepared in advance by the teacher.
- 1 scorecard for each team and a master scorecard for the teacher.
- Paper and pencils for each team.

GAME STEPS

Preliminaries
- Divide class into teams of three to six players each.
- Have each team sit at its own table.
- Distribute one scorecard to each team. (You may have to remind players to work silently.)

Round 1
- Announce *par,* the minimum number of clues needed to correctly identify the item the clues refer to.
- Present the first clue.
- Charge each team 1 *stroke* for this clue.

- Have each team write down its response on its scorecard.

- Review each team's response.

- If the response is correct, this completes the team's round.

- If the response is incorrect, team continues to play.

- Present clues until all teams have identified the item or all clues have been given.

- Post the number of strokes for each team.

Round 2 to End of Game

Play is the same for each round.

End of Game

- Tally all the team scores.

- The team with the *lowest* number of strokes wins.

SCORING EXAMPLE

Preliminaries

- Preparing Problem Sets for the Game

- The teacher of a sixth-grade class of twenty-eight students selects six concepts and events important to his lesson plan. The lesson plan covers eighteenth-century history, specifically, the American colonies. The focus is the worsening relations between the colonial governments and Great Britain.

- The teacher develops a set of five to seven facts for each concept or event.

- The first event he chooses is the Boston Tea Party. He selects these notable facts (presented in abbreviated form): December 16, 1773; Boston harbor; 340 chests of tea; forty to fifty "Indians"; British East India Company; tax on tea.

- The teacher writes out each fact as a clue.

- He sequences the clues so as to present the information in a particular order, with the most difficult clue first and the easiest clue last:

  Date: December 16, 1773

  Target: British East India Company

  Place: Boston Harbor

  Action: Raid by forty to fifty "Indians"

  Reason: Tax on tea by British East India Company

  Result: 340 chests of tea thrown into harbor

- The teacher establishes par by estimating the number of clues it should take to establish a critical mass of information—enough information to allow the average student to determine the identity of the item. He sets par at 3.

- The teacher prepares his other five problem sets in a similar fashion and then sequences these problem sets for the whole game, putting the easier problem sets first. This allows the students to understand the flow of the game before encountering more challenging material.

- The teachers divides the class into five teams of five to six players each.

- Each team meets at its own table.

- The teacher distributes one scorecard and paper and pencils to each team.

- Each team enters its name on its scorecard.

- The teacher announces that par for the first concept is 3 and posts "Par = 3" on the chalkboard.

Round 1

- Clue 1 (stroke 1)

  - The teacher reads the first clue: "Date: December 16, 1773."

  - The teams record their responses on the "Stroke 1" line of the "Round 1" section of the scorecard.

  - The teacher charges each team 1 stoke.

  - The teacher visits each table and reviews the responses.

  - No one has identified the concept.

- Clue 2 (stroke 2)

  - The teacher reads the second clue: "Target: British East India Company."

  - Teams record their responses on the "Stroke 2" line of the scorecard.

  - The teacher charges each team 1 stroke, for a total of 2 strokes.

  - The teacher reviews the responses.

  - Team A has correctly identified the Boston Tea Party. Team A has now completed this round.

  - The four other teams are still playing.

- Clue 3 (stroke 3)

  - The teacher reads the third clue: "Place: Boston Harbor."

  - The teams record their responses on the "Stroke 3" line of the scorecard.

  - The teacher charges each team still playing 1 stroke, for a total of 3 strokes.

  - The teacher reviews the responses.

  - Teams C and E have correctly identified the Boston Tea Party. These teams have now completed this round.

  - Two teams are still playing.

- Clue 4 (stroke 4)

    - The teacher reads the fourth clue: "Action: Raid by forty to fifty 'Indians.'"

    - The teams record their responses on the "Stroke 4" of the scorecard.

    - The teacher charges each team still playing 1 stroke, for a total of 4 strokes.

    - The teacher reviews the responses.

    - Teams B and D have correctly identified the Boston Tea Party.

    - The teacher goes over the final clues for this event, elaborating as necessary on the reason for and result of the Boston Tea Party.

Scoring

● The teacher posts the master scorecard with the Round 1 scores:

Round	Par	Team				
		A	B	C	D	E
1	3	2	4	3	4	3
2	4					
3	3					
4	3					
5	4					
6	4					
Total Strokes	21					

TEACHER NOTES

- Consider introducing this game by comparing it to a riddle or treasure hunt. Explain that the class will be given one clue at a time to the answer and that each team can take a guess after every clue—just like solving a mystery.

- This game brings material to life by presenting pieces of information one at a time to the student, like a breaking news story.

- This game encourages students to make the effort to identify a concept or event even when they still have less than all the available information, and rewards those teams who understand the importance of the first and second clues, which are usually the more remote or difficult ones.

- Compared to most of the other games, this game requires a different sort of thinking, not only on the student's part but also on the part of the teacher. At first, you may find writing clues difficult, but once you begin you will discover a flow inherent in the material.

- We suggest this recipe as a starter:

  - Focus on one teaching point.

  - Develop a set of facts that provide details about the teaching point.

  - Arrange these facts in a specific order.

- Here are some ways to order the clues:

  - Most difficult to most simple.

  - Earliest dates or times to most recent dates or times.

  - Most obscure to most obvious references.

  - The five "W"'s and "H"—who, what, where, when, why, and how.

- This game uses scoring similar to that employed in the game of golf. Each clue (each opportunity to identify the selected item) counts as a stroke, and the total number of strokes required for the round is compared to par, the minimum number of strokes likely to be needed. Thus the game can made less competitive by focusing play against par or more competitive by focusing it against other teams' scores.

- Use a noisemaker to announce that the teams are about to take the stroke (hear the clue) that will bring the current stroke total to par. This will increase the game atmosphere and advise the players that they should be able to identify the concept or event at this point.

- This game gives students a safe place to take chances or educated guesses. Because the environment is friendly and they are not penalized for incorrect guesses, they may feel freer to take risks and engage in critical thinking.

- By changing par, you can use the same material for different levels of students. If a class solves the clues quickly, reduce par. If another class is having trouble solving the clues, increase par.

- When you use this game to introduce a new concept or topic, increase par to compensate for the unfamiliarity of the material.

- For younger students: Allow them to keep their own scores to reinforce math skills.

- For older students:

  - Create a golf environment, using terms such as *birdie* (getting the answer in one stroke less than par) and *bogie* (getting the answer in one stroke more than par).

  - Create different *opens,* or tournaments, to cover different materials, such as the "Math Open" or the "History Open." By announcing the upcoming tournament, you will encourage students to research the material to help their teams win.

  - Allow older students to keep their own scorecards, as players do in real golf. Require all teams to turn in their scorecards at the end of play, and check them against the master scorecard.

- To expand the number of rounds, make additional copies of the scorecards with the lines renumbered, from 8 through 14.

CUSTOMIZING KNOWLEDGE GOLF

Size of Group

- For one player:

  - Have the player compete against an established par for a limited number of rounds.

  - Have the player establish her own par in the initial game. Then have her try to improve on that personal par in future games.

  - Use this game to hold an ongoing tournament in various topics, such as math, history, spelling, and science.

  - Have the student compare her progress on different *golf courses*—such as the Math Course and the Science Course. Tutoring can then focus on "improving her game" for the next tournament in her weaker topic.

- For a very small group of three or four:

  - Have all the players play as one group.

  - Call the group a *threesome* or *foursome,* as in golf, and have each player compete against the other players.

- For large groups: Divide the class into four or five teams. Have each team pick three or four players to represent it for one round. Then it picks a new set of players for the next round and so on, rotating through all the team members.

Time of Play

- Shorten or lengthen the amount of time allowed for the play of a round.

- Expand or contract the number of rounds in a game.

- Keep students in the same teams, and have them work at lowering their scores over a period of time, such as a month.

- Conduct an end-of-semester *tournament* and post the scores of each team, noting teams that have best scores, show the most improvement, and so on.

Focus of the Task   Have each team select an *observer.* When you announce the correct
response, it is the observer's job to determine whether the response
to a clue is correct.

Scoring

- Establish a *handicap*—a number of strokes to be deducted from
  each team's total—when introducing new or more challenging
  topics. For example, when introducing concepts in algebra with
  this game, you might give each team a handicap of 5 to be
  deducted from the team's score after a set of nine rounds.

- Use varying handicaps to level the playing field when teaching
  students from different grades the same material.

Knowledge Golf

Team _____

Round 1	Par _____

Stroke 1 _____
Stroke 2 _____
Stroke 3 _____
Stroke 4 _____
Stroke 5 _____
Stroke 6 _____
Stroke 7 _____

Round 4   **Par** _____

Stroke 1 _____
Stroke 2 _____
Stroke 3 _____
Stroke 4 _____
Stroke 5 _____
Stroke 6 _____
Stroke 7 _____

Round 2   **Par** _____

Stroke 1 _____
Stroke 2 _____
Stroke 3 _____
Stroke 4 _____
Stroke 5 _____
Stroke 6 _____
Stroke 7 _____

Round 5   **Par** _____

Stroke 1 _____
Stroke 2 _____
Stroke 3 _____
Stroke 4 _____
Stroke 5 _____
Stroke 6 _____
Stroke 7 _____

Round 3   **Par** _____

Stroke 1 _____
Stroke 2 _____
Stroke 3 _____
Stroke 4 _____
Stroke 5 _____
Stroke 6 _____
Stroke 7 _____

Round 6   **Par** _____

Stroke 1 _____
Stroke 2 _____
Stroke 3 _____
Stroke 4 _____
Stroke 5 _____
Stroke 6 _____
Stroke 7 _____

- Form two or more teams.

- Write down par on your scorecard.

- After the teacher presents the first clue, write your response next to "Stroke 1."

- Show the teacher your response.

- Scoring is as follows:

  A *correct* response ends your round and your team is charged 1 stroke.

  An *incorrect* response continues your play, and your team is charged 1 stroke and will be charged additional strokes until it identifies the item.

- The team with the lowest score wins the game.

LIGHTNING ROUND

INTRODUCTION   Lightning Round, an out-of-chair game played by two or more teams, asks students to practice performing under time pressure and gives you an opportunity to discuss this fact of life as well as to review topic material. The players on each team respond to a series of questions in thirty seconds. In addition to earning 3 points for each correct response, the team earns a 10-point bonus for answering all the questions correctly within the time limit.

Purpose	• To increase comfort level and confidence during standardized tests.
	• To build capability in responding promptly.
Game Objective	To score the most points.
Players	5 or more. *Can be adapted for one-on-one tutoring.*
Time	10–25 minutes.
Grades	2–8.
Supplies	• 1 set of 7 very short questions per team, per round.
	• Timer or stopwatch.
	• Noisemaker (whistle or call bell) (optional).

GAME STEPS

Preliminaries
- Divide class into two or three teams.
- Select first team to play lightning round.

Round 1: Thirty seconds
- Read the first question to the first player on the first team up.
- The team responds or *passes*.
- Read the next question to the next player.
- Continue this process until the team has responded to all the questions or thirty seconds has expired.
- If the team passed on any question(s) and time remains, reask the passed question(s).

Scoring	A *correct* response = 3 points
	An *incorrect* response = 0 points
	A *pass* = 0 points
	Bonus: Correct responses to all 7 questions = 10 points

Round 2 to End of Game

Each round is played in the same fashion.

End of Game

The team with the most points is declared the winner.

SCORING EXAMPLE

Preliminaries

- The class is divided into three teams—Team A, Team B, and Team C.
- The teacher informs the teams:
  - They have thirty seconds to respond to seven questions
  - Any player from the team may respond, but the teacher will take the first response as the team's response.
- Team A is selected to go first.

Round 1: Team A

- The team A players line up in a single line facing the teacher.
- The teacher presents the first question.
- A player responds correctly.
- The teacher presents the second question.
- No one knows the response. Team A passes.
- A player responds correctly to the third question.
- A player responds incorrectly to the fourth question.
- A player responds correctly to the fifth and sixth questions.

- The teacher calls time and tallies the score for the correct responses to questions 1, 3, 5, and 6: 4 correct responses × 3 points = 12 points.

- The teacher posts Team A's score on the chalkboard.

- This ends play for Team A for Round 1.

Round 1: Team B
- The team B players line up in a single line facing the teacher.

- A player responds incorrectly to the first question.

- A player responds correctly to the second question.

- Team B passes on the third question.

- A player responds correctly to the fourth, fifth, and sixth questions.

- A player responds incorrectly to the seventh question.

- The teacher repeats the third question.

- A player responds correctly.

- The teacher calls time and tallies the score for the correct responses to questions 2, 3, 4, 5, and 6: 5 correct responses × 3 points = 15 points.

- The teacher posts Team B's score on the chalkboard.

- This ends play for Team B for Round 1.

Round 1: Team C
- The team C players line up in a single line facing the teacher.

- A player responds correctly to the first, second, and third questions.

- Team C passes on the fourth question.

- A player responds correctly to the fifth and sixth questions.

- Team C passes on the seventh question.

- The teacher presents the fourth question again.

- A player responds correctly.

- The teacher presents the seventh question again.

- A player responds correctly.

- The teacher calls time and tallies the score for the correct responses to—all seven questions: 7 correct responses $\times$ 3 points = 21 points.

- The teacher awards the 10-point bonus for answering all seven questions correctly, giving Team C a total of 31 points.

- The teacher posts Team C's score on the chalkboard.

- This ends play for Team C for Round 1.

TEACHER NOTES

- This game allows you to use a quiz show format to review information with your students. Because some information may get "lost" in the excitement of play, you may want to go over the questions and correct answers at the completion of each round to reinforce them.

- Ask the students to comment on how their team formed and performed *under fire*. This can be an excellent opportunity to discuss team learning and team play.

- Require that a variety of team members provide one response in every round. For smaller teams, try to have each member provide one response in every round. This ensures involvement of all team members.

- Have the playing team line up in single file. After the first player responds or passes on a question, have the next player step forward. This player responds to the passed question of the previous player or to a new question.

- This format introduces a more dynamic climate and ensures player participation. Teams may even request a planning period to establish their lineup for the next round of play.

- Assign students to monitor the time and record the scoring for questions. This is one way to involve students who may not want to respond to questions in front of the entire class.

- Introduce a music track from a CD or cassette tape as the time limit for a round. This will encourage the involvement of the entire class, not just the playing team, throughout the game. Be sure to use the same sound track for each team during a round.

- Select music that may not be ordinarily heard by your students in order to introduce them to this music.

- The time pressure may frustrate some students. Talk with them or bring up the issue in a group conversation in the classroom. Having time pressures is a fact of life in many areas—school, work, even play (many sports games are timed). Let the students know that you understand their frustration and anxiety but that practice does allow them to familiarize themselves with timed situations. Let children practice with this game format before playing it for points.

- Hand out a new reading to each team. Allow the teams five minutes to read the material. Then conduct two or three rounds of this game on these new topics. This is an exciting way to introduce new material for take-home assignments.

- Conduct two or three rounds on the day following a take-home reading. This is a wonderful way to reinforce the importance of the readings. Because students do not like to let down their teammates, you can bet that even if they do not read the first assignment with you use this game, they will read future take-home assignments.

- For older grades:

  - Enlist a student from each team to read the questions. You maintain control by stating whether the response is correct or not.

  - Have the players compute their own scores; this will reinforce the application of elementary math skills.

- For larger groups: Divide the entire class into three teams and have each team select a different player lineup for each round. Be sure to run at least two rounds so that every student has a chance to play a round.

CUSTOMIZING LIGHTNING ROUND

Size of Group
- For one player:

  - Have the player estimate the score he will get, and then have him respond to seven questions in thirty seconds.

  - Establish a standard score, and then have the player try to match or exceed this score in several rounds of seven questions.

  - Have the player respond in writing to a written set of questions with a three-minute time limit. This will help him prepare for written examinations.

- For two or three players: Have each player compete against the other player(s) in separate rounds of seven questions apiece. For three players, this would require three sets of questions.

- For larger groups: Subdivide each team into two or three groups. Have each subgroup represent the whole team for one round, and then record their results as the team's score.

Time of Play
- Shorten or lengthen each round to correspond with the level of the topic and audience. You might keep the thirty-second time limit for older groups, but extend the time to one or two minutes for younger groups.

Focus of the Task
- Vary the questions by using different question formats, including short answer, true or false, and multiple choice.

- After completion of a round, allow nonplaying teams to respond—either in writing or orally—to any questions missed by the playing team.

Scoring

- Penalize a team 1 point for any wrong response.

- Change the bonus scoring to a staggered system:

  3 consecutive correct responses = 3 points

  5 consecutive correct responses = 7 points

  7 consecutive correct responses = 10 points

  2 incorrect responses = stop play

SCORE SHEET
Lightning Round

Round	Team	Team	Team
1			
2			
3			
4			
5			
Total Points			

Lightning Round

- Form two or three teams.

- The teacher presents the first of seven questions.

- If team's response is

    Correct, move to next question.

    Incorrect, move to next question.

    Pass, return to question at end if time permits.

- Round ends when thirty seconds expires or when the team has responded to all seven questions, whichever comes first.

- Scoring is as follows:

    A *correct* response = 3 points

    Bonus: Correct responses to all 7 questions = 10 points

- Once all rounds are finished the team with the most points wins.

MEDLEY RELAY

INTRODUCTION   Medley Relay, an out-of-chair or even outdoors game played by two or three teams, takes some time to set up and play but rewards you with very high levels of player involvement. Academic skills and motor ability are equally important here, and children are continually challenged to mix these capabilities. Each team undertakes a medley of tasks: a Trash Ball toss, a Test Battery, a relay Balloon Walk, a Pass Around of assorted objects, and a Lightning Round of questions. The object is to complete the tasks in as little time as possible. Correct responses to topic questions allow teams to deduct some time from their scores.

| **Purpose** | • To involve students in applying the topic to problems. |
| | • To exercise motor skills and academic skills simultaneously. |

Game Objective   To complete the tasks in the minimum amount of time.

Players   10 or more. *Can be adapted for one-on-one tutoring.*

Time   25–50 minutes.

Grades   4–8.

Supplies
- 1 set of 7 Test Battery and 17 Lightning Round questions per team, prepared in advance by the teacher.
- 10 wadded papers and a round trash can.
- 6 or more inflated balloons.
- 1 set of 6 objects dissimilar in weight and size, such as a plastic gallon jug, empty egg carton, roll of tape, balloon, chalkboard eraser, lunch bag stuffed with crumpled papers, tennis shoe, batting helmet, tennis ball, Ping-Pong ball, and so forth.
- A stopwatch.
- Paper and pencils for players.
- A noisemaker (optional).

GAME STEPS

Preliminaries
- Divide the class into two or three teams of five players or more.
- Have each team meet to select players to complete these specific tasks:

- Trash Ball—one player

- Test Battery—three players

- Balloon Walk—two players

- Pass Around—five players

- Lightning Round—entire team.

Round 1

- Task 1: Trash Ball.

  - One player shoots wadded papers at a trash can until she makes three baskets.

  - Scoring: Time spent on task.

- Task 2: Test Battery.

  - Three players respond to a battery of seven questions.

  - Scoring: Time spent on task minus 10 seconds for each correct response.

- Task 3: Balloon Walk.

  - Two players, performing one at a time, walk a set course while keeping a balloon in the air.

  - Scoring: Time spent on task.

- Task 4: Pass Around.

  - Five players form a circle and pass around six objects without dropping any of them.

  - Scoring: Time spent on task

- Task 5: Lightning Round.

  - Any player on the team may answer questions in 30-second period.

  - Scoring: Time spent on task minus 3 seconds for each correct response.

Scoring

- Total the score for Round 1 as follows:

  Trash Ball = Time spent on task

  +

  Test Battery = Time spent on task

  Number of correct responses × −10 = Time deducted

  +

  Balloon Walk = Time spent on task

  +

  Pass Around = Time spent on task

  +

  Lightning Round = Time spent on task

  Number of correct responses × −3 = Time deducted

  Total time spent (in seconds)

- Post the time on chalkboard.

Round 2 to End of Game

Each round is played in the same fashion.

End of Game

The team that completes the task medley in the shortest time wins.

SCORING EXAMPLE

Preliminaries

- The class is divided into two teams.

- The teacher plans to conduct one round for each team.

Round 1: Team A

- Task 1: Trash Ball: A trash can is placed seven feet from a marked line. The player stands behind the marked line and is supplied with ten wadded sheets of paper, or *trash balls*. The player's task is to throw three trash balls into the trash can. The turn is over when the player has made three *baskets*.

  - The teacher starts Task 1.

  - The Team A player makes three baskets in 20 seconds.

  - The teacher records 20 seconds on the chalkboard.

- Task 2: Test Battery: The teacher has three Team A players meet at the front of the class. She explains that any member of the trio may respond to a question, but that is the only response allowed. The team must respond to seven questions.

  - The teacher starts Task 2, presenting one question at a time.

  - The three Team A players respond to the seven questions, taking 55 seconds and getting six correct.

  - The teacher records 55 seconds on the chalkboard, noting that the team made six correct responses for later scoring.

- Task 3: Balloon Walk: A fifteen-foot lane is established with a line or marker at each end. The two players stand at one end of the lane. Each player must walk to the end line *and* back while successfully keeping the balloon in the air. If the balloon is held or dropped, the player must start over.

  - The teacher starts Task 3.

  - The first Team A player walks the balloon to the end line and back, then hands off the balloon to the next player. He takes 25 seconds.

  - The second player walks the balloon to the end line, but drops the balloon when he turns around. He goes back to the starting line and restarts his walk. He completes the walk this time. He takes 45 seconds.

  - The total time is 25 + 45 seconds.

  - The teacher records 70 seconds on the chalkboard.

- Task 4: Pass Around: Five players form a circle. The teacher gives each player one item. In addition, one player gets an item called the *marker*. The items are an empty plastic milk container, a chalkboard eraser, an egg carton, a tennis shoe, and a tennis ball. A roll of duct tape is the marker.

  The teacher tells the group to pass all six of the items around the circle. The task is completed when the marker has been passed around for two complete cycles. If any player drops any item, the team must restart the task.

  - The teacher starts Task 4.

  - The team begins passing the items.

  - After one successful cycle the chalkboard eraser is dropped.

  - The team restarts and successfully passes all the items around two complete cycles.

  - The total time taken is 50 seconds.

  - The teacher records 50 seconds on the chalkboard.

- Task 5: Lightning Round: The teacher has the entire team line up at the front of the class. The teacher explains that any member of the team may respond to a question, but that is the only response allowed. The team has 30 seconds to respond to as many questions as it can.

  - The teacher starts Task 5, presenting one question at a time.

  - Team A responds to ten questions. Five of the answers are correct.

  - The teacher records 30 seconds on the chalkboard, noting that there were five correct responses for later tallying.

Scoring for Team A Round 1

Task 1:	Trash Ball	=	20 seconds
Task 2:	Test Battery	=	55 seconds
	6 correct responses $\times -10$	=	-60 seconds
Task 3:	Balloon Walk	=	70 seconds
Task 4:	Pass Around	=	50 seconds
Task 5:	Lightning Round	=	30 seconds
	5 correct responses $\times -3$	=	$\underline{-15 \text{ seconds}}$
			150 seconds

The teacher posts this score: Round 1: Team A = 150 seconds.

TEACHER NOTES

- This game is more complicated in setup and play than any of the other games in this book. But the payoff is truly worth it. This game can celebrate the end of a teaching module or a special occasion. The activity and the competition associated with each task will keep your class riveted to the proceedings.

- Consider having more than one adult to monitor the activities. The monitor's task is to observe the game, help keep track of the scoring, and keep the teams on task. For grades 6 to 8, consider using student monitors. Have a quick training session to prepare your monitors so they know what to look for and do during the game.

- Allow teams to designate *specialty players*—players selected to perform specific tasks. You may want to keep this selection process within the team—if you appointed a trash ball thrower and he does poorly, for example, this may cause dissension.

- Establish a best time from previous play and select an *all-star* team to try to better that time. Have the rest of class act as scorekeepers and monitors for the event.

- Be sure to review all question material after each round to clarify and elaborate on the correct responses.

- Use this game to demonstrate the mix of motor and academic skills needed in the real world, from balloon walkers to test takers. Players with varied skills are all to be valued by their teammates.

- Entertain student suggestions for items to be used in playing Pass Around. This not only empowers the students but will also substantially increase your list of eligible items.

- Allow teams time to practice the motor skill tasks, especially Pass Around and Balloon Walk. This might be the time when teams see which players have the specialty skills needed for some specific tasks.

- Springtime and the end of the year can be very difficult times to keep students on task. This is a perfect game to take outside. Children will be outdoors, exercising their motor skills while reinforcing their academic skills—what could be more perfect than that?

CUSTOMIZING MEDLEY RELAY

Size of Group

- For one player:

    - Eliminate the Pass Around task.

    - Have the player complete the remaining four tasks against an standard time, such as three minutes.

    - Use the player's best time as a time to beat in future competitions.

- For groups smaller than ten: Have one team play against an established standard or against its own best time.

- For larger classes: Divide the group into three teams. Expand the number of players who participate in Balloon Walk and the number of items and players for Pass Around.

Time of Play	• To shorten the game, omit or shorten a task. Require only one Balloon Walk (back and forth), for example, or only one cycle of Pass Around.
	• To lengthen the game, add a task, expand a task, or increase the number of players in the task.
Focus of the Task	• Take the game outdoors, and add other tasks such as a soccer ball kick and real basketball shooting. This can be very productive at those times of the year when keeping students on task is especially challenging.
	• Increase the number of motor skills tasks, with another type of target throw, for example.
	• Increase the academic tasks by introducing another type of oral quiz, such as a spelling or arithmetic bee, or by including a timed paper-and-pencil quiz that is to be handed in and scored upon completion.
	• For older students: Add a new level of difficulty to the motor skills games. Require the Balloon Walk players to hop on one foot or to bounce the balloon off their heads, for example.
Scoring	• Increase or decrease the bonus for correct answers to Test Battery and Lightning Round questions.
	• Award a bonus to any team that completes Pass Around or Balloon Walk without a dropped item.
	• Award a bonus to any team that completes the medley in less than a specified time.

Medley Relay

	Team	Team	Team
Task 1 Trash Ball	Time _____	Time _____	Time _____
Task 2 Test Battery	Time _____ − # Correct × 10 _____ = _____	Time _____ − # Correct × 10 _____ = _____	Time _____ − # Correct × 10 _____ = _____
Task 3 Balloon Walk	Time _____	Time _____	Time _____
Task 4 Pass Around	Time _____	Time _____	Time _____
Task 5 Lightning Round	Time _____ − # Correct × 3 _____ = _____	Time _____ − # Correct × 3 _____ = _____	Time _____ − # Correct × 3 _____ = _____
Total Points			

- Form two or three teams.

- Your team must complete these tasks in the least amount of time that it can:

  Task 1: Trash Ball

  Task 2: Test Battery

  Task 3: Balloon Walk

  Task 4: Pass Around

  Task 5: Lightning Round

- The teacher computes the time the team required to perform each task and posts the total.

- After all rounds are completed the team performing the tasks in the least time wins.

MUSIC TIME

INTRODUCTION   Music Time can introduce children to music they might not ordinarily hear, and if the teacher wishes, it can also bring a random element to game timing. The first team lines up single file, and the teacher begins a musical selection. Each player must respond to his or her question before the next question can be presented to the next player. The team's turn, and chance to win points, ends when the music stops. Beating the clock is more exciting when one isn't sure when the clock will stop. Other fun methods can also be used to time games randomly.

Purpose	• To introduce students to accomplishing academic tasks within random time periods.
	• To expose students to forms of music they may not hear elsewhere.

Game Objective	To score the most team points.

Players	10–40. *Can be adapted for one-on-one tutoring.*

Time	15–35 minutes.

Grades	3–8.

Supplies	• A set of questions on the topic, prepared in advance by the teacher.
	• Audio player.
	• CD or tape cassette with musical clips or selections, all of approximately the same duration (at least initially).
	• Stopwatch or kitchen timer.

GAME STEPS

Preliminaries	• Divide the class into two or three teams.
	• Each team responds to as many questions as it can until the musical selection ends or until time is called.
	• Each player must respond to his or her question before the next player is eligible.

Round 1: Team One
- Have the first team line up in single file.
- Start a musical selection.
- Present the first question to the first player.
- The player must give a response.

Scoring

A *correct* response = 1 point

An *incorrect* response = 0 points

- Present the second question to the second player.
- Play continues in this fashion until the musical selection is complete.
- The teacher calls time.
- The teacher tallies the total number of points and posts the score on the chalkboard.

Round 2 to End of Game

Each team plays its round in a similar fashion.

End of Game   The team with the most points is declared the winner.

SCORING EXAMPLE

Preliminaries
- The class is divided into two teams—Team A and Team B.
- Team A lines up in a single file.
- The teacher starts the musical selection on the audio player.

Round 1: Team A

- The teacher presents the first question to the first player.
- The first player responds correctly.
- Team A earns 1 point.
- The teacher presents the second question.
- The second player responds incorrectly.
- Team A earns 0 points.
- The round continues in this fashion until the musical selection ends and the teacher calls time.
- Team A has made nine correct responses.
- The teacher tallies the score and posts it: Round 1: Team A = 9 points.

Round 1: Team B

- This half of the round is played in a similar fashion.
- Team B makes eleven correct responses.
- The teacher tallies the score and posts it: Round 1: Team B = 11 points.

TEACHER NOTES

- What a wonderful way to introduce different forms of music to children of all ages. This game allows you to bring the "Mozart effect" into your classroom and give your children an opportunity to hear music they might not hear outside the classroom.

- Random version: preprogram randomly timed musical selections, with shorter and longer segments. To neutralize complaints about other teams getting longer selections, have students draw straws for turns. The randomness of the self-selection will reinforce the spirit of play.

- Longer versions (music-while-you-work):

  - Begin a five- to ten-minute musical selection and hand out written question or problem sheets to groups at their own tables. Have each group work on the questions or problems during this randomly timed music. The music induces a calming atmosphere while still creating uncertainty about the time the students have to accomplish the task. If the children become familiar with a specific selection and time their work accordingly, you will have successfully introduced them to this musical form.

  - Hand out a new reading to each team. After a short period, hand out a set of questions on the readings. Allow the teams to work on responses to the questions during the rest of the musical selection. When the music stops, have each team hand in one response sheet, and then go over the questions and answers with the class.

- Use longer musical selections to calm down your class after an energetic recess or assembly.

- Be sure to go over all the questions and responses after a round of play to elaborate on and reinforce the correct responses.

- Allow teams to meet before their round to establish a sequence of players to answer the questions.

- Allow older students to compute their own scores. This empowers the learning and could surface issues of fairness and honesty.

- Set a time limit of five to fifteen seconds for each response to ensure that any player who freezes and cannot respond does not sabotage an entire team's score.

- Assign one or two students to assist you in setting up the musical selection, keeping track of the correct and incorrect responses, and computing the scores.

- You may change this game so it focuses only on the random element and not on music. Create random *time tasks,* and present questions until they end. We are sure you will have several favorites of your own, but here are some starter suggestions:

- Blow a bubble, and present questions until it pops.

- Have the players in a team stand on one foot. Questioning continues until one of them loses his balance.

- Have the players in a team stand in a circle and keep several balloons in the air. Questioning continues until they drop one of the balloons.

- Have one member of a team shoot wadded paper balls at a trash can. Questioning continues until the she misses one or two shots.

- Have two members of a team do a *double throw* until one of them drops one of the objects and ends the question period. (The two players, each one holding a different object, toss them simultaneously to each other. For instance, player A holds a tennis ball, and player B holds an egg carton. Then they each toss their object to the other player, simultaneously requiring a toss and a catch.)

- Have team members build a tall, thin structure of blocks. Have one player pull out one block for each question asked. Questioning continues until the structure collapses.

- Keeping track of correct responses during play.

  - If you are reading the questions from a question list, you may want to mark a "C" by each correctly answered question. This will help you tally the correct responses at the end of the round. It will also tell you which question material is giving your students the most trouble. You may consider restating questions missed in earlier rounds to reinforce the learning.

  - If you are reading questions from index cards, you may want to place the discarded questions into *correct* and *incorrect* piles to make it easier to tabulate the points and reuse missed questions.

CUSTOMIZING MUSIC TIME

Size of Group

- For one player:

  - Compare the player's tally to a previous score made by the player.

  - Have the player respond to a written set of questions in the set time period. This will help him prepare for timed examinations.

- For three to five players:

  - Have the players form a team and stand in a single line facing the teacher. Present a series of questions in the time allotted.

  - Give the players a beanbag and have them pass the bag in a *hot potato* fashion around the group. The player left *holding the bag* when time is called must answer the next one or more questions.

Time of Play

- Shorten or lengthen each round to correspond with the amount of time you wish to devote to the topic, question format, or the age of the audience.

- Vary the cues that signal the end of the round, such as a musical segment, then a buzzer, then a random but specific noise (a cough from the next room) occurs.

- Have the team respond to questions while one of the team members performs a random time task as described earlier.

- Use a noisemaker to signal the end of the round; it immediately gets everyone's attention and adds to the game atmosphere.

Focus of the Task

- Vary the questions by using different question formats.

- When using preprogrammed music, have teams draw straws so they take their turns in random order.

- Inform teams they may keep playing until they make an incorrect response or no response to a question.

- Use a longer musical selection and have groups of players work on a question or problem sheet, as described earlier.

Scoring

- For older audiences or *challenge rounds,* award 1 point for each correct response and subtract 1 point for an incorrect response or no response.

- Award a bonus point for every consecutive correct response. Thus a team that gives six consecutive correct responses receives a 6-point bonus.

- At the end of one team's turn, allow other teams to select and respond to questions missed or not responded to during the round. Award or penalize the other teams 1 point, in accordance with the correctness of each response.

SCORE SHEET

Music Time

Round	Team	Team	Team
1			
2			
3			
4			
5			
Total Points			

- Form two or three teams.

- The first team lines up in single file.

- The teacher starts a musical selection.

- The teacher presents a question to the first player. (The player must respond before next question can be presented.)

- Scoring is as follows:

  A *correct* response = 1 point

  An *incorrect* response = 0 points

- When the music stops, the team's turn is over.

- At the end of the round the teacher tallies all points and posts scores.

- After all rounds have been played the team with the most points wins.

Scavenger Hunt

INTRODUCTION   Scavenger Hunt helps students learn by sharing information, and you might also use it in the first week of school as an icebreaker, helping students get to know one another. The game sheet typically lists characteristics students might have or asks for items of information about a topic. Individual players get the signatures of students who have a characteristic or who know an item of information. The player who correctly identifies the most items wins. Many variations can be introduced to make the game appropriate for a specific classroom.

| **Purpose** | • To foster social interaction and sharing of knowledge. |
| | • To reinforce understanding of the topic. |

| **Game Objective** | To complete the game sheet. |

| **Players** | 4 or more. *Can be adapted for one-on-one tutoring.* |

| **Time** | 15–45 minutes. |

| **Grades** | 2–8. |

| **Supplies** | • Game sheets, one for each player. |
| | • Paper and pencils for players. |

GAME STEPS

Preliminaries	• Develop one set of characteristics or clues related to things that students will hunt for.
	• Create a game sheet by listing the clues.
	• Make copies, one for each student.

A Complete Game	• Distribute one game sheet to each player.
	• Give players ten minutes to complete the game sheet by obtaining *autographs* from other students who meet the requirements of the characteristics.
	• Validate the completed game sheets of the first three players to finish (optional).
	• Call time after ten minutes.

End of Game

- Review the game sheet by calling on players who have signed for specific characteristics.

- The first three players with completed game sheets win (optional).

SCORING EXAMPLE

Preliminaries

- This is the first day of class, and the teacher develops a short game sheet of clues about the upcoming curriculum. She hopes that in the spirit of play the students will collaborate with each other to solve the clues.

- Each player receives a game sheet (as shown here), and players are told they have ten minutes until time is called.

Scavenger Hunt

Directions

- Read this list and get a signature of a student who

  - Meets the requirement of the item *or*

  - Knows the correct response to the item.

- You are limited to one signature from each class member.

- When you have completed the list, hand it in to your teacher for validation.

1. Has a Rod Stewart CD. _____

2. Can name the author of the book *Great Expectations.*
   Author _____
   Student _____

3. Plays on an organized sports team. _____

4. Can name the capital city of Belgium.
   City _____
   Student _____

5. Has a pet lizard or snake. _____

6. Can name the chemical formula for water.
   Formula _____
   Student _____

7. Plays the trumpet or saxophone. _____

8. Can name one of the four elements of the First Amendment.
   Element _____
   Student _____

9. Collects baseball or sports cards. _____

10. Can name the country in which the play *Hamlet* takes place.
    Country _____
    Student _____

A Complete Game

- Students seek out others who might fill a requirement listed or know the answer to a statement.

- After a few minutes, one or two students approach the teacher with a game sheet they feel is completed. The teacher reviews the game sheet and makes the appropriate comments. If the sheet is complete, the teacher initials it.

- After ten minutes, the teacher calls time.

- The teacher reviews the game sheet, asking for volunteers who signed off on each requirement to share information with the class.

- For a personal item, the teacher asks the student identified with the characteristic to elaborate (what CD, what kind of snake, and so forth). For an academic item, the teacher asks the students who knew the answer to comment on the item or else the teacher elaborates on the item, as necessary.

TEACHER NOTES

- This familiar *icebreaker* game gives you an exciting, classroom-tested format that you can use with almost any audience and topic. The game sheets are easy to prepare and serve as an excellent way for students to make and keep topic notes.

- An exciting discovery game, Scavenger Hunt can be used with any topic and at any time of the day. When your students have completed the game sheets, be sure to go over the content to reinforce the learning.

- Use this game to have students demonstrate their baseline skills in the existing curriculum or in a new topic.

- This game can be played in several formats:

  - Single player (in class): The student receives a copy of the game sheet and solves as many clues as he can. To create a desk version or learning center activity, prepare game sheets using only academic clues.

- Single player (at home): The student takes home a game sheet filled with academic clues and solves as many as she can. You can review the solutions in class or have the students form groups and then share and compare their solutions. Take-home Scavenger Hunt can reinforce both take-home reading and classroom discussion.

- Team play: Each student receives a copy of the game sheet and meets with other players to solve as many clues as the group can. This format can be played seated or students can get out of their chairs in the search for the personal and academics items listed.

  - Hand out game sheets as homework. The next day, have students form teams to think, pair, and share their findings. This will encourage completion of homework assignments and underscore the ongoing curriculum.

  - Hand out game sheets, call for a short period of individual work, then bring students into teams to share and compare their findings.

  - Hand out game sheets and immediately bring students into teams to share the workload.

  - Have teams complete as much of the list as they can from their desks before looking for other students to sign off on items.

- Bingo format: Clues are arranged on a grid, like a five-by-five Bingo game card, and students are asked to get enough signatures to fill up a line of boxes horizontally, vertically, or corner-to-corner. This format is quicker than others to set up and complete. A team may be asked to seek signatures from other teams or to try to cover five spaces in a row with team members' own signatures. (See the sample and blank game sheets for Scavenger Hunt Bingo at the end of this game.)

- Wall game sheet: Post an oversized version of the game sheet on the bulletin board, and ask students to volunteer items that match a theme, such as "my favorite TV show," or to solve one of the clues and then sign their name. Review this game sheet at the end of the period or day. This version encourages students to respond to requests for information in moments of open time. (See the sample sign-up game sheet at the end of this game.)

- "Who Am I?": This version uses a "Who Am I?" question format to elicit short written answers about curriculum items. For example:

  I am your "host" in the famous novel *Moby Dick*.

  I am the value of a in the problem: $a^2 + 5 = 9$.

  I share the longest border with the United States.

  I am the current Prime Minister of Great Britain.

- Turn the completed game sheet into programmed notes by structuring the clues to follow the week's curriculum. Distribute the game sheet the first day of the week, and have the students work on it throughout the week. They might for example, solve clues about the terms in algebra as they discover those terms from the classroom work. Go over the solutions on the final day of the curriculum to elaborate and clarify, as required. What a wonderful way to create notes about the topic.

- Similarly, design a game sheet that complements a single day's lecture about a topic. Have each team mark its game sheet when the players hear an item on the sheet mentioned or see it shown. Again, with this game students prepare their own structured classroom notes for the lecture.

- Create a balance in the game items by mixing topic-related and generic, fun items. This mix of game play and subject recall can be used for audiences of any size, ranging from tutoring sessions of two or three students to larger classroom groups.

- Use this game as a mini–field trip activity by writing "Who Am I?" clues about objects placed around the playground or in the auditorium or gym.

- Use this game on an actual field trip to reinforce many of the learning points to be found on the trip.

- For larger groups: Use monitors to help you validate individual or team game sheets.

CUSTOMIZING SCAVENGER HUNT

Size of Group

- For one player: Prepare a list of academic clues.

    - Fixed time: Have the player identify as many solutions as possible in a limited time.

    - Open time: Have the player try to complete the entire game sheet.

- For small groups: Prepare a list of academic clues, divide the children into two teams, and have them compete against each other.

- For larger groups:

    - Conduct single player versions. Give each student a game sheet, and have him solve as many clues as he can.

    - Split the class into sections. Have one team play a set of games while the other teams watch. Review the results of the game with the entire class.

Time of Play

- Vary the time according to the grade level and topic.

- Use as an ongoing activity. Have students store the game sheets in their desks, and seek answers to the clues for an entire week.

- Speed up the game by allowing players to sign one or two spaces as "free," meaning they do not have to answer or respond to that space, allowing more freedom and faster game play.

Focus of the Task

- Use as a single-player icebreaker for new classes or for students to share what they did on vacation. In this version, students seek out other students who fit the characteristics described and have them sign for the appropriate ones.

- Write the clues at the appropriate level of difficulty for each class.

- For small groups: Create lists of academic clues.

- For larger groups: Create one academic clue for every "find someone who" clue, for a pleasant mixture of intergroup discovery and topic reinforcement.

- Use a foreign language version to demonstrate and reinforce usage of that language. (See the sample sheet for a Spanish Scavenger Hunt, with instructions in English and Spanish, at the end of this game.)

- Have students begin a game at home and then share and compare with teammates the next day.

- Allow players to sign one of the lines in their own game sheet if they fill the description or know the answer.

Scoring

- Reward the first five individuals or the first two or three teams who complete their game sheets.

- Award 1 point for each completed item. Increase the points for more difficult clues.

Spanish Scavenger Hunt

Instrucciones

- Esta actividad requiere que te obtengas informacíon de otras personas.

- Busca a alguien en el cuarto que tenga los requisitos de una de las categorias.

- Tú puedes obtener sola una firma de cada participante.

- Tú necescitas cumplir cuatro de las cinco categorias para terminar la actividád.

- Tú puedes usar tu propia firma para cualquier topico.

- Cuando has terminado la forma enseñesela a su instructor.

Instructions

- This activity requires you to obtain information from others.

- Find someone in the room who meets the qualification(s) of one of the categories.

- You are allowed to obtain only one signature from any one participant.

- You need to complete four of the five categories to complete the task.

- You are allowed to use your own signature for any one topic.

- When you have completed the form, show it to the instructor for validation.

1. Ha estado eseñando por más de 10 años. _____

2. Ha vivido en otro país seis meses o más. _____

3. Usa juegos o otras actividades en las clase. _____

4. Puede decir "rubber baby buggy bumpers" rapidamente, tres veces. _____

5. Usa una computadora personal en su trabajo. _____

SAMPLE GAME SHEET

Scavenger Hunt Bingo

Directions   Fill in five spaces in a row—horizontally, vertically, or corner-to-corner—by getting the signature of a student who meets the requirement for each statement.

You are limited to one signature from each class member.

When your list is completed, turn it in to your teacher for validation.

Has three or more brothers or sisters	Plays a musical instrument	Plays on a sports team	Lives in an apartment	Walks to school
Has a dog	Sings in a choir	Roller blades	Ice skates	Can "sight read" music
Lifts weights	Jogs	Wears contacts	Has read the *Harry Potter* books	Plays tennis
Has a bird feeder	Tap dances	Has been to Disneyland or Disney World	Was born west of the Mississippi	Can speak a second language
Surfs the Net	Water skis	Plays lacrosse	Is a left- hander	Is a twin

Scavenger Hunt Bingo

Directions Fill in five spaces in a row—horizontally, vertically, or corner-to-corner—by getting the signature of a student who meets the requirement for each statement.

You are limited to one signature from each class member.

When your list is completed, turn it in to your teacher for validation.

Scavenger Hunt

Rules of Play

- Player may contribute one or more ideas.

- Player must enter each new idea on a numbered line.

- Player must write his or her name or identifying initials.

- Teacher may call on a student to explain why this is his or her favorite show.

Brainstorm Topic: My Favorite TV Show

Show	Name
1. "Who Wants to Be a Millionaire?"	Emanual Martin
2. "Malcolm in the Middle"	Eric Berringer
3. "The Simpsons"	Mike Roberts
4. "King of the Hill"	Dillon Glyder
5. "Cops"	Steve Gaffney
6. "Ally McBeal"	Colleen Ritagold
7. "Hollywood Squares"	Jennifer Frawley
8. "Seinfeld"	Dick Kalt
9. "Wheel of Fortune"	Mike N. Dawn
10. "Dharma and Greg"	Clarisse Ragus
11. "Whose Line Is It?"	Luke Copeland
12. "The Drew Carey Show"	John Brooks
13. "Star Trek: Voyager"	Greg Steven
14. "Rosie O'Donnell"	Katie Victor
↓	
25.	

Scavenger Hunt

- Receive a copy of the game sheet.

- Find someone who

  Meets the requirement of an item *or*

  Knows the correct response for the item.

- Ask the person to sign off on the requirement or write down the correct response.

- When time is called, the teacher will go over the solutions.

Spin Off

INTRODUCTION

Spin Off adds variety to the topic review process and also gives students some math practice. Playing at a table or on the floor, groups of students spin a bottle or spinner to take random turns at responding to a question presented by the teacher. This game also reveals the collective value inherent in a team. Each player in each group selects a team color. At the end of the game, the tokens collected by players for the Red Team, the Blue Team, and the Green Team are separately totaled and the players on those teams suddenly discover how many more points the team has than any individual has.

| **Purpose** | • To build understanding of information and data. |
| | • To initiate discovery of the value of a team. |

| **Game Objective** | To collect the most tokens. |

| **Players** | 4 or more. *Can be adapted for one-on-one tutoring.* |

| **Time** | 15–45 minutes. |

| **Grades** | K–8. |

Supplies	• 1 set of questions, prepared in advance by the teacher.
	• 1 empty plastic 2-liter bottle for each table.
	• 1 paper cup and 1 set of 10 to 15 tokens or chips per table.
	• 1 set of *tent cards* (1 red, 1 green, and 1 blue) at each table. The tent cards are 5-by-8-inch index cards folded in half, with each side of the tent marked with the color red or green or blue using felt-tipped marker or colored dots.

GAME STEPS

Preliminaries	• Divide class into groups of four to eight players each.
	• Have each group meet at a table.
	• Have each player select a red or green or blue tent card and then place it in front of him. The colors on the tent cards designate different teams (Red Team, Green Team, and Blue Team).
	• Place one paper cup with a set of chips in it on each table.
	• Place one plastic bottle on its side on each table.

Round 1	• Have one player spin the plastic bottle.
	• The player closest to the bottle mouth when the bottle stops must respond to a question presented by the teacher.
	• If there is a tie, the player spins the bottle again.
	• The teacher presents the first question.
	• The answering player gives his response to the rest of the players at the table.

Scoring	For a *correct* response the player takes 1 chip from the cup
	For an *incorrect* response the player gets 0 chips.
	The answering player then spins the bottle.

Round 2 to End of Game

Play is the same for all rounds.

End of Game	• Have players count their chips and then add up the chips for all the players on each team at each table.
	• The team with the most chips at each table is declared the winner.

SCORING EXAMPLE

Preliminaries	• The class divides into groups
	• Each group sits at a table with a paper cup and chips, one empty plastic two-liter bottle (on its side), and one colored tent card identifying each player's team—the Red Team, the Green Team, or the Blue Team.

Round 1, Table A
- The teacher announces the first round of play.
- One player at Table A spins the plastic bottle.
- The mouth of the bottle points to a player on the Green Team.
- The Green Player must respond to the first question.
- The teacher presents the question.
- The Green Player states her response to the rest of the table.
- The teacher presents the correct response.
- The Green Player was correct and takes 1 chip from the container.
- This completes play for Round 1.

Round 2, Table A
- The Green Player spins the plastic bottle.
- The mouth of the bottle points to a player on the Red Team.
- The Red Player must respond to the second question.
- The teacher presents the question.
- The Red Player states his response to the rest of the table.
- The teacher presents the correct response.
- The Red Player was incorrect.
- The Red Player does not earn a chip.
- This completes play for Round 2.

Scoring
- Play continues in this fashion until the end of the game.
- The players at the table count their tokens individually and then add together the tokens for each team.
- The Green Team has 5 chips, the Red Team has 4 chips, and the Blue Team has 3 chips.
- The Green Team has the most chips and is declared the winner.

TEACHER NOTES

- This game underscores both individual achievement and the *collective value* of a team. By adding their chips together, players learn that a team is more than just a collection of players.

- Another way to reinforce the collective value concept is to tally all the chips in all the groups won by each team. This would demonstrate that it took the chips from all a team's players in all the groups to equal the winning total. Thus, if the Red Team's winning total was 12 chips, those winning chips might have represented 4 chips from the Red Players in one group, 3 chips from the Red Players in a second group, and 5 chips from the Red Players in yet a third group.

- This is both an academic and a tactile game. Players not only respond to question material but touch, collect, and count their chips.

- The spinning of the bottle and team play keeps all players involved on every new spin.

- You may have to address the issue of students yelling out the answers and using overheard answers as their own.

- Vary the number of chips awarded with the difficulty of the question. Also consider penalizing players for wrong responses; this may increase the competition in the game.

- For younger students:

  - For conducting several games, consider using volunteers or teaching assistants.

  - Play the game on the floor. This will lead to a more relaxed and playful atmosphere and avoid the problem of having the bottle roll off the table.

  - Reread questions aloud and go over the correct responses with the class.

  - Hold up picture clues and go over the correct responses with the class.

- For older students: Outside the classroom, students conduct many of their own games. This is a good game to use for bringing student creativity and leadership into an in-class game. Empower groups with the responsibility to conduct major elements of the game, from judging correct responses to awarding chips, to conducting the final tally of chips and proclaiming the winner. If successful, this self-monitoring approach could translate into more student empowerment in other facets of classroom activities.

  - Assign one student to each group to act as game monitor, question reader, and awarder of chips.

  - The questions can be printed on index cards and placed in the middle of the table. The student leading the game at that table then draws cards and reads the questions aloud to the players.

  - Older students can also contribute questions for game play.

- Use objects other than a bottle. Let your students create other spinnable objects. Give this assignment for homework and let them bring in their *inventions*. The winning inventions can be used during actual game play. Note that for reasons of safety, teachers of younger students may not want to use a glass bottle. Middle school teachers may want to stay away from using any kind of bottle because it is likely to recall the kissing version of the game to the students ("Spin the Bottle").

- A popular variation is the *tennis ball* version of this game. Hand each group a tennis ball. Allow the students to pass the ball around, until you blow a whistle or make some other sound and announce, "Stop." The player holding the ball at that point must respond to the question. You can observe which students are not participating and call a stop when one of these students is holding the ball.

CUSTOMIZING SPIN OFF

Size of Group

- For one player: Create a game sheet by drawing a large circle with numbers or categories in the quadrants (as shown here) and placing it under the bottle. The number that the mouth of the bottle is pointing to when it stops indicates the point value or the category of the question that will be asked.

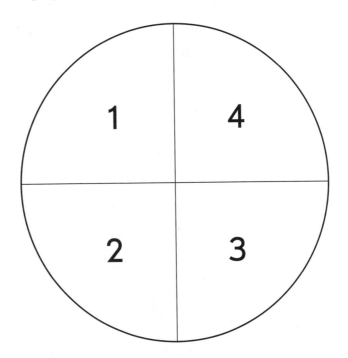

- Time driven: Have the student collect as many points as possible within a one-minute period.

- Quantity driven: Have the student attempt to match or exceed a specific score.

- For small groups: Have them play either as one group or individually in the one-player versions of the game.

- For large groups:

  - Conduct several games simultaneously. Review the results of each question and the game results with the entire class.

  - Split the class into sections. Have one section play a set of games while the other section watches. Review the results of the game with the entire class.

Time of Play

- Lengthen or shorten the time limits for responses, depending on size of the group or difficulty of the question.

- Play for a specific length of time or number of rounds.

Focus of the Task

- After the bottle points to a player from a specific team, allow the team to select any of its players to respond to the question.

- If the spinner points between two players, have both respond to the question at the same time. Each player can write down an answer or quietly convey it to an observer, monitor, or nearby player.

- Create one set of question cards for each group. Have the player to the left of the answering player read the question.

- Take this game outside during nice weather. It can be played with students seated on the grass or the playground.

- Assign a number to each player at the table. Use a master spinner mounted on an overhead transparency or placed on the teacher's table (in full view of the class). The player at each table whose number is indicated by the spinner answers the next question.

- Replace the spinner with a tennis ball, as described earlier.

- Have one table spin the bottle for the rest of the class. For example, when the mouth of the bottle points to a Red Player at the table, a player of that color at all the tables must respond to the question. Rotate this assignment so that each group has a chance to be the representative table.

- *Fishbowl* the game by having only one table play the game. Have each player represent a team from the class so everyone is represented at the table. Either rotate the players at the table or allow the entire team to participate in the answer.

Scoring

- Assign each question a point value, and have the player take the specified number of chips from the cup.

- Assign point values to each question, and post ongoing scores on the chalkboard.

- Play a *put-and-take* version in which an incorrect response puts 1 or more chips into the cup and a correct response takes 1 or more chips.

Spin Off

- Divide into groups.

- Each group meets at a table.

- Each player selects a team color and places a card with that color in front of him or her.

- One player spins the bottle.

- The player closest to the mouth of the bottle must respond to the question presented by the teacher.

- Scoring is as follows:

  For a *correct* response the player takes 1 chip from the cup.

  For an *incorrect* response the player gets 0 chips.

- At the end of the game, the team with the most chips wins.

THREE-IN-A-ROW

INTRODUCTION   Three-in-a-Row is a perfect first classroom game because its Tic-Tac-Toe format is already familiar to some students and others can learn it instantly. Two teams play on each Tic-Tac-Toe game sheet. The first team selects a square and then responds to a question. If the answer is correct, the team covers the square with a token or a mark. Play continues this way, alternating between the teams, until one team covers three squares in a row. Try this game in one of its several variations as a review right after a reading or as a bridge between a very active period and seated classroom work.

Purpose	• To improve topic comprehension by becoming involved with the topic.
	• To introduce the concept of game play and of combining games with learning.

Game Objective	To cover 3 squares in a row.

Players	2 or more. *Can be adapted for one-on-one tutoring.*

Time	20–45 minutes.

Grades	K–8.

Supplies	• A set of questions, prepared in advance by the teacher.
	• 1 Tic-Tac-Toe game sheet for each pair of teams.
	• 2 tokens, such as chips of different colors or different coins, for each game sheet.
	• Paper and pencils for players.

GAME STEPS

Preliminaries	• Divide the class into several sets of two teams—the X Team and the O Team.
	• Distribute one game sheet, two tokens, and a pencil to each set of teams.
	• Select one team to start.

Round 1: X Team

- The X Team selects a square on the game sheet by placing its token on that square.

- The teacher presents the first question.

- The X Team gives its response to its opponents.

Scoring

For a *correct* response, the X Team removes its token and covers the square with an "X."

For an *incorrect* response, the X Team must remove its token.

Play alternates to the O Team.

Round 2

- The O Team selects a square and places its token on it.

- The O Team gives its response to its opponents.

Scoring

For a *correct* response, the O Team removes its token and covers the square with an "O."

For an *incorrect* response, the O Team must remove its token.

The first team to get three "X"'s or "O"'s in a row wins.

TEACHER NOTES

- The simplicity of this game, known to all as Tic-Tac-Toe, allows for an almost immediate understanding of how the game is played—allowing students to become instant players and focus immediately on questions about the topic in a play-and-answer format. This user-friendly dynamic makes the game a strong candidate for a classroom's first game. Imagine introducing a game and presenting your questions within five minutes.

- This is a great game for reinforcing reading comprehension. Use the game to wrap up a read-aloud or book reading period.

- This game not only engages the students in the information but also enhances strategy skills through the game play. You may find that students will want to continue playing the game after you have used up your content questions.

- Use this game immediately following highly active periods, such as recess, to encourage students to engage in a much calmer game play dealing with the current curriculum.

- This game can add the variety of game play to subject recall during tutoring sessions with two or three students.

- Create one or more sets of questions on index cards to use with the game sheet. Use the cards in these situations, for example:

  - For small groups: Allow the players to use these questions to conduct the game themselves. This will build their multi-tasking capability as they follow directions, read the questions, and respond to the topic.

  - For rainy days: Use this game as a quiet play game on rainy days when you have an indoor recess. Give your students a break from the usual curriculum and have a set of question cards ready with age-appropriate trivia for these recess games. Ask students to contribute their own questions on recent movies, music, and current events. Make sure you preview these questions to ensure their appropriateness.

  - For a learning center: When some students are done with regular classwork and others are still working, those who are finished can go to a quiet corner to play this game until the period ends. This rewards students who finish their work yet still reinforces the topic through game play.

  - For special play: Keep a file folder or bin with spare game sheets and sets of question cards on various topics. Write the set topic on each set of cards so you can list on the chalkboard those topics the students can use during play. This will help promote independence in your students.

- For younger children:

  - Have students play the traditional Tic-Tac-Toe game to become more familiar with the concept of game play.

  - Read the questions aloud or hold up a picture.

  - Go over the questions in more depth and give more one-on-one attention.

- For older children:

  - Allow them to self-monitor this game. This will build their independence as they take charge of their own learning activity.

  - When students conduct their own games, issues of fairness may arise over such incidents as covering a square when a response was not correct. This is an excellent opportunity to discuss the real-life issue of cheating but in a nonthreatening way.

  - As described earlier, ask students to contribute questions about movies, music, and current events. Then mix the best of these questions with topic-related questions. This mix is a surefire way to keep student interest.

- Consider laminating the game sheets for more durability and having the players use water-based felt-tipped markers. A simple wiping of the game boards at the end of the day will restore them for future use.

- Use a noisemaker to announce when a team covers three squares in a row.

CUSTOMIZING THREE-IN-A-ROW

Size of Group

- For one player:

    - Time driven: Have the player fill as many squares as he can before a three-minute time period runs out. As the player becomes more proficient, shorten the time period to two minutes, then one minute.

    - Quantity driven: Have the player try to fill the entire game sheet in a longer time period, such as seven minutes.

- For small groups: Have groups of two to four divide into teams and play on one game sheet.

- For larger groups:

    - Conduct several games simultaneously. Review the results of the game with the entire class.

    - Split the class into sections. Have one section play a set of games while the other section watches. Review the results of the game with the entire class.

Time of Play

- Set time limits within which teams must answer their questions.

- Play for a specific length of time or number of rounds.

Focus of the Task

- Number the columns—1, 2, and 3—and create three different categories of questions. (See the three-topic version of the game sheet at the end of this game.) In selecting a square, a team also selects the category of the question that will be asked.

- Use the four-square version of this game (see the sample game sheet) and expand play to three teams, awarding 5 points for getting three in a row and 15 points for getting four in a row.

- Play teacher versus class. Assign one game sheet per team. Have one team select a square for all the teams. Present a question. All teams that respond correctly cover the square. Then the teacher selects a square and flips a coin. If she gets heads, it counts as a correct response, and she covers the selected square. If she gets tails, it counts as an incorrect response. Play continues until a team or the teacher gets three in a row.

- Play without tokens. Have players place a finger on the square they wish to cover and keep it there during the presentation of the question. This involves the player tactilely. It is also a solution when tokens are unavailable.

Scoring

- Vary the difficulty of the questions.

- Allow students to cover the center square only if they respond correctly to two questions or respond to a more difficult question. Then award 1 point for covering an outside square and 2 points for covering the center square. Total the score at the end of each round of play.

- Play the tournament version. Have teams play a series of games. Award 1 point for each covered square, 2 points for covering the center square, and a 5-point bonus for getting three in a row. The first team to reach 21 points wins.

Three-in-a-Row

Three-in-a-Row
Three-Topic Version

Topic #1	Topic #2	Topic #3

Three-in-a-Row

Two Points for Center Square Version

Three-in-a-Row
Four-Square Version

- Divide into sets of two teams each.

- The first team selects a square and places its token on the square.

- The first team responds to a question.

- Scoring is a follows:

  For a *correct* response, the team removes its token and covers the square with an "X" or an "O."

  For an *incorrect* response, the team must remove its token.

- Play alternates to the other team.

- The first team to cover three squares in a row wins.

TRASH BALL

INTRODUCTION   Trash Ball employs both academic and motor skills and shows that both are important. Players toss a wadded paper ball, or "trash ball," at a round trash can and, if the ball goes into the trash can, respond to a question. The team receives points based on both the correctness of the response and the accuracy of the toss. This active game is especially good for special days, and with some attention to the mix of questions, children of different ages can play this game together.

Purpose	• To allow those inclined toward academics and those inclined toward athletics to share success in the same game.
	• To improve topic knowledge and practical math ability.
Game Objective	To score the most team points.
Players	2 or more. *Can be adapted for one-on-one tutoring.*
Time	10–45 minutes.
Grades	K–8.
Supplies	• A set of questions about the topic, prepared in advance by the teacher.
	• 3 or more sheets of paper, wadded into paper balls.
	• 1 round trash can.
	• Masking tape.

GAME STEPS

Preliminaries	• Use masking tape to make a shooting line—the line from which players will toss the trash balls at the target.
	• Set up a trash can two or three steps away from the shooting line. (If you want the players to have an easier time making baskets, place the trash can next to a wall. This allows shots that would otherwise go wide to bank off the wall and into the trash can.)
	• Divide the class into two or three teams.
	• Have each team line up in single file.
	• Select one of the teams to go first.

Round 1	• Have the first player toss a trash ball at the trash can.
	• If the trash ball misses the trash can, bring the next team up to start its turn.
	• If the trash ball goes into the trash can, announce a basket and present a question to the player.

Scoring

A *correct* response = 3 points

An *incorrect* response = 1 point

Round 2 to End of Game

Play is the same for each round.

End of Game   Teams tally their scores. The team with the highest score wins.

SCORING EXAMPLE

Round 1: Team A
- The first player from Team A tosses the trash ball.
- The ball goes in the trash can.
- The teacher presents a question.
- The player's response is correct.
- The teacher awards 3 points to Team A:

	Team A
Round 1	3

Round 1: Team B
- The first player from Team B tosses the trash ball.
- The ball goes in the trash can.
- The teacher presents a question.
- The player's response is incorrect.
- The teacher awards 1 point to Team B:

	Team A	Team B
Round 1	3	1

Round 2: Team A
- The second player from Team A tosses the trash ball.
- The ball misses the trash can.
- This ends Team A's turn:

	Team A	Team B
Round 1	3	1
Round 2	0	

Round 2: Team B
- The second player from Team B tosses the trash ball.
- The ball goes in the trash can.
- The teacher presents a question.
- The player's response is incorrect.
- The teacher awards 1 point to Team B:

	Team A	Team B
Round 1	3	1
Round 2	0	1

TEACHER NOTES

- This is another game that gets children out of their seats yet still focuses on learning. It is also a good game for reinforcing kinesthetic learners and visual learners.

- This game involves a mix of physical and intellectual skills. Some children who are lagging behind in their studies may be very skilled athletically. This game will give them a chance to shine and to feel good about their skills.

- The scoring system shows students that all skills are valuable in the classroom and in life—that athletic ability and book smarts work together to get the job done. Both skills are valued, as is each individual person in the classroom for the unique skills that person brings to the group. A wonderful lesson about life.

- This is a fun game for "special days"—those days before a long vacation, or day that has a school assembly or class party. This game also may be used on those days when students seem to have difficulty sitting down to their regular work.

- This is also a good game for younger grades, even if reading skills are not yet developed. Through oral questions and responses, the student is reinforced in the meaning of the question and the appropriateness of the correct response.

- This game reinforces the concept that energy is a good thing and that classrooms are good places to expend that energy.

- Create a more complete basketball environment by doing any or all of the following:

  - Introduce this game at a time corresponding with the first games or the play-offs in the college or professional basketball seasons.

  - Create a *foul line* and have the shooter and the shooter's entire team stand behind the line.

  - Create numbered shirts for all the players on each team by writing numbers on half sheets of paper and taping a number onto each player's back.

- Create an ongoing league with four or more teams and keep a won-lost record for the *season*. Nonplaying teams can become spectators in the *bleachers*. If successful, establish a play-off schedule.

- Create programs that identify each player on a team and that player's number. Use this in conjunction with the ongoing league described above.

- Invite other classes to watch a play-off game if appropriate.

- For younger students: Keep the group small. If possible, keep the rest of class busy with an assistant, and then switch the sections.

- For older students: Encourage them to keep their own *shooting percentage.* This is a practical way to reinforce the use of math and statistics in everyday life. The shooting percentage is simply the number of successful tosses divided by the total number of attempts. If a student attempts a total of 12 tosses and makes 8 of them, his shooting percentage is 8 divided by 12, or 66 percent.

- For multiage, multigrade classrooms: Mix the difficulties of the questions to allow children of different ages to compete in the same game.

- For large classes: Try to get a *referee,* perhaps a parent volunteer or teaching assistant, to control the crowd. Another person is always helpful for control and perspective when the students' energy and activity level is raised.

- Create a series of questions in increasing difficulty. Use the easier questions in the first round, and increase the complexity of the questions in each subsequent round.

- Play practice games to allow the students to understand their roles and the rules of the game.

- Look in your classroom recycling bin for paper to use in the game. This sets an example for your students about preserving resources and using what's available.

- Place the trash can against a wall to see if this *backboard* makes it easier to make the basket. Ask if there are any ways the children can create personal backboards to help them with seemingly difficult problems.

CUSTOMIZING TRASH BALL

Size of Group

- For one player:
  - Have the player earn as many points as possible in seven tosses.
  - Establish a standard number of points per toss—such as 2 points—and have the player match or better the standard. For a game of seven questions then, the player's goal is 14 or more points.
  - Have the player establish her own standard and then try to match or better that score.
- For larger groups: Have one set of teams play at a time while other teams observe.

Time of Play

- Shorten or lengthen the time period allowed to respond to the question.
- Play to a predetermined number of points. The first team to match or better this predetermined score wins.

Focus of the Task

- Allow the player responding to a question to confer with or receive coaching from his team.
- Set up two trash cans, one closer to and one farther from the shooting line. The farthest target earns 5 points for a basket plus a correct response.
- Set up two trash cans of different sizes. The smaller target earns 5 points for a basket plus a correct response.

- Set up two shooting lines, one nearer to the target and the other one step farther back. The farthest shooting line earns 5 points for a basket plus a correct response.

- Allow all the players on a team one shot each at the target. Total the baskets, and then present the same number of questions to the team.

- Place the trash can on a chair.

- Vary the size of the target in accordance with the age of the player. For younger children, use trash cans or laundry baskets. For older children, use a number 10 can or the equivalent (a five-pound coffee tin or forty-six-ounce juice can).

Scoring

- Award 1 point for either answering the question or making a basket. Award a 1-point bonus for making both a correct response and a basket, for a total of 3 points.

- Designate a Lightning Round. Each team selects one player who shoots as many paper balls at the target as possible in fifteen seconds. Then use one of the following question methods:

  - Present one question: a correct response wins as many points as the player made baskets. An incorrect response receives 0 points.

  - Ask the team a series of questions, with the number of questions equal to the number of baskets, awarding 2 points for each correct response and 0 points for each incorrect response.

- Hold a face-off: Pose a question to both teams. Have each team toss at the basket. The first team to make a basket when its opponent misses the basket responds to the question. A correct response scores 3 points, and an incorrect response earns 1 point.

- Award a 7-point bonus to the team that correctly responds to all questions.

- Award a 5-point bonus to the team that makes baskets on all of its tosses.

Trash Ball

0 points = Missed toss (no basket)
1 point = Made toss (basket)
3 points = Made toss and gave correct response

Round	Team	Team	Team
1			
2			
3			
4			
5			
6			
7			
8			
Total Points			

Trash Ball

- Form two or three teams.

- Line up in single file.

- The first player on the first team tosses a trash ball at the trash can.

- If the player misses, the next team comes up to play.

- If the player makes a basket, the teacher presents a question to the player.

- Scoring is as follows:

  A *correct* response = 3 points

  An *incorrect* response = 1 point

- After all rounds have been played, the team with the most points wins.

PART THREE

Finding the Right Game

APPENDIX **ONE**

GAME SUMMARIES

Here is a brief summary of each game, indicating significant features of play and special requirements. Use these summaries to find just the right game to meet the needs of your students' learning styles, learning types, and the curriculum area you want to address on a particular day. Once you have identified your game, proceed to the game description, which details what you need to do to prepare and play the game in your classroom.

Activity Cards (Card Game)

This is an in-chair or out-of-chair card game played by two or more teams. Each team has sixty seconds to collect as many points as it can. The teacher draws a card designating the point value of the upcoming question, and then she reads the question to the players. If team members answer correctly, the team collects the amount of points shown on the card. Play continues until time expires or a "Stop Play" card is drawn, and then play moves to the next team. The game comes with reproducible game cards.

Alphabet Soup (Prop Game)

This is an out-of-chair game or table game played by two or more teams. Each team receives a set of letter cards and then has three minutes to form words of two or more letters using those cards. A team's total points are determined by the number of letters in each word formed during the round of play. The game comes with a sample word list.

At Risk (Prop Game)

This game is played at a table or on the floor by one or more small groups of students. When the teacher presents a question, the first player who thinks she knows the correct response covers her head with her hand. All other players in that group must then race to cover their heads. The last player to cover is *at risk*. If the first-to-cover player responds correctly, she collects a chip and the at-risk player loses a chip. If the first-to-cover player responds incorrectly, she loses a chip.

Balloon Juggle (Prop Game)

This out-of-chair game is played by two or more teams. The first team sends up a player who is handed one balloon. The player must keep the balloon in the air while he responds to a question. Points are awarded on the quality of the response and for keeping the balloon aloft.

Batter Up! (Prop Game)

This is a baseball-style game played by two teams. The first team sends a player, a *batter,* to respond to a question. If correct, the batter scores a *hit*. If incorrect, the batter gets an *out*. The team's players continue to respond to questions until they receive three outs. The team scores its first run on the fourth hit of the *inning* and subsequent runs on additional hits.

Bingo 1: Letter Bingo (Requires Game Sheets)

This is an in-chair game played by two or more teams. Each team receives a Bingo-style game sheet with one letter or letter group in each square. The teacher presents a clue and then each team selects the letter that represents the correct response. The first team to cover four squares in a vertical, horizontal, or corner-to-corner diagonal row wins.

Bingo 2: Math Bingo (Requires Game Sheets)

This is an in-chair game played by two or more teams. Each team receives a Bingo-style game sheet with one or more numbers in each square. The teacher presents a clue or mathematical problem, and then each team selects the number that represents the correct response. The first team to cover four squares in a vertical, horizontal, or corner-to-corner diagonal row wins.

Bingo 3: Wall Bingo (Wall Game)

This is an in-chair game played by two or three teams on a Bingo-style game sheet placed on the wall. The first team selects a point value square and then responds to a question appropriate to that point level. If the team's response is correct, the teacher covers the square and awards the team the designated points. If the team's response is incorrect, the square is left uncovered. Each team's point total is a combination of the points earned for each square covered and bonus points for covering three or more squares in a row. The team with the most points wins.

Bits and Pieces (Prop Game)

This is an out-of-chair game in which each player receives one piece of a shape and then must find other players whose pieces complete the shape. Each group of players whose shape pieces match up must then complete the task written on the completed shape. When time is called, each group reports on its task.

Bubbles (Prop Game)

This is an out-of-chair game played by two or more teams. A player from the first team responds to a question. If the response is correct, the team receives 3 blows on the bubble maker. If incorrect, they receive 1 blow on the bubble maker. The team receives 1 point for each bubble counted. The team with the most points wins.

Crosswords (Requires Game Sheets)

This is an in-chair or take-home game. Each player receives a game sheet and clue sheet and then meets with the other players on his team. Each team must solve as many items on the game sheet as it can within the prescribed time. The team that has solved the most clues wins.

Dilemma (Sorting, Wall Game)

This is an out-of-chair game played by two or more teams on game sheets placed on a wall. Each team meets at one of the game sheets, which names two or more categories. In front of the team is a series of item cards, placed face down. The first player turns over the first card and then places it under one of the categories on the game sheet. The second player turns over and plays the next card. Play continues until time is called. The team that has correctly placed the most items on the chart wins.

Fast Track (Wall Game)

This is an in-chair game played by two or more teams. Each team is assigned one track on the wall game sheet. Teams are then asked questions, with correct responses advancing the team's icon up the wall chart. The team whose icon has advanced the farthest on the game sheet wins.

Grab Bag (Prop Game, Requires Score Sheet)

This is an in-chair game played by two or more teams. Using a response sheet, each team answers a series of questions. When one or more of the teams receives 11 points, each member of those teams earns a trip to the grab bag to pull for a surprise.

Granny Squares (Requires Game Sheet)

This is an in-chair game played by two or more teams using game sheets. Before every question, the players on each team select one of the four squares they think is the one covered by the teacher. The question is then presented. The score for each round is a combination of the correctness of the response and the correctness of the square selection. Teachers may give hints about which square is covered, to reinforce directions and clue solving.

Guesstimate (Requires Game Sheets)

This is an in-chair test preparation game played by two or more teams. Each team is required to estimate the number of questions it will answer correctly. The teams then take the test. Each team's score is computed by comparing their original estimate to their actual number of correct responses. This game can be played in one or more rounds, depending on the amount of question material you wish to cover with the class.

Guggenheim (Wall Game)

This is an out-of-chair creativity game played by two or more teams on game sheets placed on the wall. Game sheets show a matrix, or grid, with letters on the horizontal axis and categories on the vertical axis. Each team develops a list of items suggested by the categories and letters for each square on the game sheet. Each team receives 1 point for each item and a 5-point bonus for placing at least one item in each square on the game sheet.

Knowledge Golf (Requires Game Sheets)

This is an in-chair clue solving game played by two or more teams. Each team must identify an item from a set of clues, given one clue at a time. The teacher establishes a minimum number of clues needed to identify the item, or *par*, and then presents the clues. Each clue counts as a *stroke*. The number of clues needed to identify the item determines each team's score. The team with the lowest number of strokes wins.

Lightning Round (Requires Timer)

This is an out-of-chair game played by two or more teams. Each team must respond to a series of questions in thirty seconds. The round ends when the team has responded to all questions or time has expired. The team earns 3 points for each correct response and a 10-point bonus if it responds correctly to all of the questions.

Medley Relay (Prop Game, Requires Set-Up, Requires Timer)

This is an out-of-chair game played by two or three teams. Each team must complete a medley of tasks that include a Trash Ball toss, a Test Battery, a relay Balloon Walk, a Pass Around of assorted objects, and a Lightning Round of questions. The time spent on each task is computed, with time deducted for correct responses made during the Test Battery and Lightning Rounds. The team completing the tasks in the least time wins.

Music Time (Prop Game)

This is an out-of-chair game played by two or three teams. Each team lines up single file and the teacher begins a musical selection. Each player must respond to his or her question before the next question can be presented to the next player. When the music stops, the teacher calls time. The team with the highest number of correct responses wins.

Scavenger Hunt (Requires Game Sheets)

This is an out-of-chair clue identification game. Each player receives a copy of the game sheet and then must complete the game sheet by identifying each item defined. The player who correctly identifies the most items wins. This game, which has many variations, can also be used as an icebreaker, team game, or take-home exercise.

Spin Off (Prop Game)

This is a game played at a table or on the floor by two or more groups. Each player in the group selects a team color and places a tent card with that color in front of him or her. One player spins a bottle or spinner. The player closest to the mouth of the bottle or arrow of the spinner when it stops spinning must respond to a question presented by the teacher.

Three-in-a-Row (Requires Game Sheets)

This is an in-chair game played by sets of two teams on a Tic-Tac-Toe game sheet. The first team selects a square and then responds to a question. If correct, the team covers the square. Play alternates to the second team. Play continues until one team covers three squares in a row. Several game sheet variations are presented with the game description.

Trash Ball (Prop Game)

This is an out-of-chair game played by two or three teams. Each team lines up in single file. The first player tosses a wadded paper ball, or "trash ball," at a round trash can. If the ball goes in the trash can, the player then responds to a question. The team receives points based on both the correctness of the response and the accuracy of the toss.

SAMPLE GAME LESSONS

We have developed sample game lessons, or game plans, to respond to two ordinary classroom challenges in the skill areas of language and math. Each game plan will work through the problem and present a working classroom game. We hope that these game plans will inspire you to create many, many games to resolve some of your own classroom challenges.

Game Plan 1: Letter Recognition—First Grade

The Challenge

It's the second week of class, and Mrs. Parker needs to find out how much her students already know about letters and the sounds they make. Because it is only the beginning of the school year, the teacher wants to prepare a low-key, low-stress form of assessment.

Mrs. Parker's goals also include having the students get to know each other while she assesses their skills at letter recognition.

The Game Plan

Mrs. Parker's game plan is to present the students with a set of words, one for each letter of the alphabet, and through a familiar paper-and-pencil game, determine how well the students recognize the sounds of the initial letters of these words.

Step 1: Develop a Set of Words

- The teacher selects these words: *apple, ball, cat, dog, elephant, fox, gate, heart, ice, jet, kite, lion, mom, no, pumpkin, quilt, red, sun, tent, umbrella, violin, water, xylophone, yak,* and *zoo.*

- She places each word on a three-by-five-inch index card.

Step 2: Assemble Pictures

- The teacher assembles as many pictures representing these words as possible.

- She places each picture on an index card.

Step 3: Select a Game Format

- The teacher selects Bingo 1: Letter Bingo because of its ease of play and familiarity to the students.

Step 4: Create the Game Sheets

- The teacher develops a game sheet (as shown here) for the words represented by pictures.

R	S	A	M
C	E	F	H
D	T	U	V
P	Q	Z	X

SAMPLE GAME SHEET

- The teacher photocopies one game sheet for every two students.

- She develops additional game sheets to use with words with or without pictures.

Step 5: Identify Steps in the Game Play

- For the first round, the teacher uses the first game sheet and the words with pictures. She reads the word aloud and then shows the picture to the students.

- For the second and third rounds, she uses the other game sheets. She reads the word aloud but shows pictures only if they are available.

- After she presents each word, the teacher writes the word on the chalkboard and elaborates as required.

- For more information about game play, please refer to Bingo 1: Letter Bingo, page 103.

Step 6: Assemble Game Supplies

- This game requires index cards, game sheets, and one marker for each team.

Game Plan 2: Geometry—Fifth Grade

The Challenge

Mr. Tuttle has just finished teaching a unit on geometry. He feels that the students may not have understood all of the material, but they were growing restless with this topic. He decides to use a game to evaluate their level of comprehension and plans to review responses after each round so that the students receive a review and additional information.

Mr. Tuttle's goals are to gently assess learning comprehension while reinforcing knowledge of two-dimensional shapes.

The Game Plan

Mr. Tuttle's game plan is to present the unit using tactile shapes in a team problem-solving exercise.

Step 1: Develop a List of Shapes

- The teacher develops a list of the shapes to be covered in the game: triangle, circle, and quadrilateral.

Step 2: Develop Set of Tasks

- The teacher develops a set of tasks for several of the shapes:

Find the area and circumference when the diameter equals ten inches.

Name four quadrilaterals with two or more equal sides.

Name four or more types of triangles.

Step 3: Select a Game Format

- The teacher selects Bits and Pieces because of its ability to bring students into problem-solving groups and to review the topic in a practical way.

Step 4: Create the Game Sheets

- For the class of thirty students the teacher prepares three shapes—circle, rectangle, and triangle—by cutting two sets of shapes from orange and green construction paper. He then writes the task on the appropriate shape and cuts each shape into five pieces. The teacher now has three shapes in green and three in orange, each shape cut into five pieces, for a total of thirty pieces for his class (see the three sample figures).

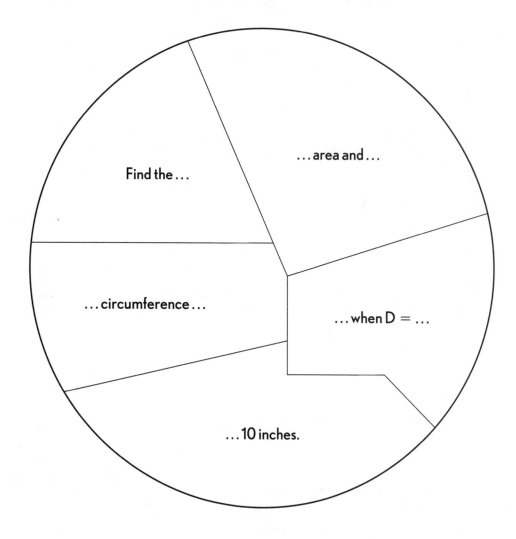

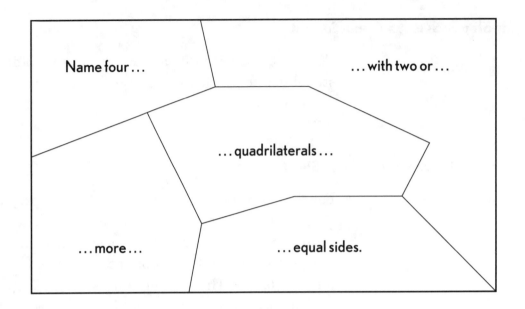

Name four . . .

. . . with two or . . .

. . . quadrilaterals . . .

. . . more . . .

. . . equal sides.

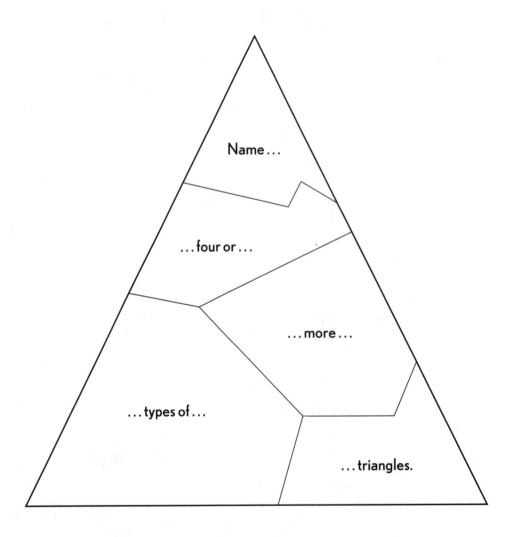

Name . . .

. . . four or . . .

. . . more . . .

. . . types of . . .

. . . triangles.

Step 5: Game Play

- The teacher introduces the task and then hands out the pieces of the shape containing the task assignments. (Today there are three absent students, so the teacher hands an extra piece of each shape to three students.)

- After the students form task groups of the same shape in green and orange, they are given five minutes to complete their task.

- At the end of five minutes, the group representing each shape reports on its task to the rest of the class.

- For more information about game play, please refer to Bits and Pieces, page 147.

Step 6: Game Supplies

- This game requires construction paper (green and orange, or two other colors), a set of marking pens, and scissors.

GAMES FOR SPECIAL SITUATIONS

Here are five classroom situations that could be problematic for any teacher, new or experienced. First, we describe each situation briefly. Then we present a grid showing suggested games for three clusters of grades.

Situation 1: First Week

It is the first week of class, and the teacher wants a way to get to know her students while finding out where they stand academically. She does not want to do anything that resembles testing and wants the class to have fun in their introduction to the subject.

Grade Level	Suggested Game	Comments
K–2	Bits and Pieces	Use first day with picture task
	Bubbles	Use outside, nice weather
	Letter Bingo	Demonstrates letter recognition
	Math Bingo	Demonstrates number recognition
	Grab Bag	Use at end of week
3–5	Bits and Pieces	Use first day with simple task
	Bubbles	Use outside, nice weather
	Letter Bingo	Word recognition skills
	Math Bingo	Simple math skills
	Three-in-a-Row	Use to review material
6–8	Bits and Pieces	Use first day with simple task
	Scavenger Hunt	Use mix of personal and academic clues
	Letter Bingo	Word and clue skills
	Math Bingo	Math skills
	Wall Bingo	TV game–format review

Situation 2: Test Preparation

Standardized tests are approaching, and the teacher wants to prepare his class in a nonthreatening way. He chooses to use a game every other day for two weeks prior to testing to help his class prepare in a productive yet enjoyable way.

Grade Level	Suggested Game	Comments
K–2	Granny Squares	Use pictures, should help directions
	Letter Bingo	Demonstrates letter recognition
	Math Bingo	Demonstrates number recognition
3–5	Granny Squares	Use first day with simple task
	Three-in-a-Row	Play in multiplayer teams
	Letter Bingo	Word recognition skills
	Math Bingo	Simple math skills
	Guesstimate	Use to review material *and* test-taking procedures (grades 4–5)
6–8	Granny Squares	Use first day
	Lightning Round	Use to introduce test "stress" factor
	Letter Bingo	Word and clue skills
	Math Bingo	Math skills
	Guesstimate	Use to review material

Situation 3: Material Review

The teacher wants to introduce new material to her class but has observed that many of her students seem to have forgotten basic skills. She decides to use games so that her students can have fun while brushing up on their skills.

Grade Level	Suggested Game	Comments
K–2	Granny Squares	Use pictures, simple letters or numbers
	Letter Bingo	Letter recognition skills
	Math Bingo	Number recognition skills
3–5	Granny Squares	Use two-player teams
	Three-in-a-Row	Play in multiplayer teams
	Letter Bingo	Word recognition skills
	Math Bingo	Simple math skills
	Guesstimate	Use to review material *and* test-taking procedures (grades 4–5)
6–8	Activity Cards	Use to encourage team learning
	Wall Bingo	Use to encourage team learning
	Letter Bingo	Word and clue skills
	Math Bingo	Math skills
	Guesstimate	Use to review material

Situation 4: Active Days

It is Valentine's Day, and the teacher knows her students will be excited from handing out Valentines and will also be looking forward to the party at the end of the day. She knows that historically this is not a productive day. This year she decides to make this day a *game day*. She plans on playing one game in the morning and then another game in the afternoon before the party. This way her students will get some work done even though they are having a hard time concentrating because of the holiday.

Grade Level	Suggested Game	Comments
K–2	Bubbles	Use to review material *and* counting skills
	Grab Bag	Use to disburse prizes at end of day
	Trash Ball	Use to reinforce material in an active way
3–5	Balloon Juggle	Use to encourage team play
	Batter Up!	Use to review material
	Bits and Pieces	Use to encourage team focus on task
	Grab Bag	Use to disburse prizes at end of day
6–8	Balloon Juggle	Use to encourage team learning
	Bits and Pieces	Use to encourage team learning
	Medley Relay	Requires setup and breakdown
	Scavenger Hunt	Use academic clue version
	Trash Ball	Use to review material

Situation 5: Learning Centers

The teacher has been having classroom management problems. Some of his students finish their work earlier than others, and the ones who finish quickly seem to distract those who are still working. He worries that he is not challenging these children enough. He decides to set up a corner of the room with games that can be student led. He prepares all the materials ahead of time and goes over the rules of the games with the students ahead of time also. Now, when any of his students finish early, they can go to the game corner, play a game, and practice their knowledge with their peers while the others are still working on their assignments.

Grade Level	Suggested Game	Comments
K–2	Dilemma	Use to practice sorting skills
	Alphabet Soup	Use simple word combinations (grades 1–2)
3–5	At Risk	Use cards with simple questions
	Alphabet Soup	Use simple word combinations
	Crosswords	Use simple word cross combinations
	Dilemma	Use to practice sorting skills
	Three-in-a-Row	Use one- and two-player versions
6–8	Activity Cards	Use to review material
	Alphabet Soup	Use to reinforce word construction
	Crosswords	Use to review material
	Guggenheim	Use to encourage creativity
	Scavenger Hunt	Use academic clue version
	Three-in-a-Row	Use to review material

Game Match Matrix

This section matches each game against a set of seven educational goals and game dynamics that define your classroom or home-schooling situation. First, we comment briefly on each of the seven characteristics. Then we present the Game Match Matrix, a table that allows you to instantly check the characteristics of any game in this book.

Grade Level

Although all the games in this book have been written and adapted for grades K through 8, the grade range indicated in the matrix is the *ideal* grade range for each game.

Curriculum

Except for two games designed to be used for language arts and one game designed for math study, all games in this book can be adapted for use with any topic in your curriculum. You will find tips on how to adapt any game to your topic in Chapters Two and Three and Appendix Two.

Group Size

The size of your class will affect the way your game is prepared and played. Some of our games work more smoothly with small groups, while other games require you to break your class into two or three groups. You will find tips on how to adapt games to your class size in Chapter Two and in the discussions of the individual games. In addition all of our games can be adapted for use with one player for the home-schooled child.

In or Out of Chair

Some games in this book encourage your students to be active and mobile (out-of-chair games)and some are played primarily by children seated at their desks or tables or on the floor (in-chair games). You might, for example, wish to select a low-key in-chair game on a "low-energy" day and an out-of-chair game on "high-energy" days when you want your students to be more actively involved.

Special Day

Special days are those times when teachers may have difficulty keeping their students on task—the day before or following a vacation, the final days of school, and the day of or just after a sweet tooth holiday such as Halloween or Valentine's Day. To keep the students focused on curriculum on these days, the matrix recommends eight games that allow your children to participate in particularly playful activities that also reinforce your topic.

Learning Center Activity

Some of our games can be easily adapted for use as learning center activities for individuals or small groups. Such activities provide an additional challenge and motivation for children who finish their assigned work early, allowing them to stay on task while their classmates complete the regular work.

Time of Play

This column of the matrix shows the amount of time recommended for game play (in minutes).

GAME MATCH MATRIX

Game	Grade Level	Curriculum	Group Size	In or Out of Chair	Special Day	Learning Center Activity	Time of Play (Minutes)
Activity Cards	3–8	All	All	In		Yes	15–45
Alphabet Soup	1–7	Language Arts	Small	Out		Yes	15–45
At Risk	3–8	All	Small	In		Yes	10–30
Balloon Juggle	2–8	All	All	Out	Yes		10–30
Batter Up!	3–8	All	Medium-Large	In and Out	Yes		15–45
Bingo 1: Letter Bingo	K–8	Language Arts	Small-Medium	In			15–45
Bingo 2: Math Bingo	K–8	Math	Small-Medium	In			15–45
Bingo 3: Wall Bingo	3–8	All	All	In			20–45
Bits and Pieces	K–8	All	Small-Medium	Out	Yes		15–30
Bubbles	K–5	All	Small-Medium	Out	Yes		15–35
Crosswords	3–8	All	Small	In		Yes	20–45
Dilemma	K–8	All	Medium-Large	Out		Yes	15–30
Fast Track	3–8	All	All	In and Out			25–50

Game	Grade Level	Curriculum	Group Size	In or Out of Chair	Special Day	Learning Center Activity	Time of Play (Minutes)
Grab Bag	K–8	All	All	In	Yes		15–45
Granny Squares	K–8	All	Small-Medium	In			15–45
Guesstimate	4–8	All	Small-Medium	In			25–45
Guggenheim	3–8	All	Small-Medium	Out		Yes	15–40
Knowledge Golf	3–8	All	All	In			20–35
Lightning Round	2–8	All	Medium-Large	Out			10–25
Medley Relay	4–8	All	Medium-Large	Out	Yes		25–50
Music Time	3–8	All	Medium-Large	Out			15–35
Scavenger Hunt	2–8	All	Small-Medium	Out	Yes	Yes	15–45
Spin Off	K–8	All	Small	In			15–45
Three-in-a-Row	K–8	All	Small	In		Yes	20–45
Trash Ball	K–8	All	All	Out	Yes		10–45